VEDIC
EAS

MW01258045

Anatoly Malakov

Vedic Astrology- Easy& Simple Copyright © 2021 by Anatoli Malakov

All rights reserved. No part of this publication may be reproduced, distributed, or transmitted in any form or by any means, including photocopying, recording, or other electronic or mechanical methods, without the prior written permission of the publisher.

ISBN 978-619-188-579-4 (e-book)
ISBN 978-619-188-578-7 (paperback)

Publisher- Anatoli Malakov

Contacts:
Email:
astrology.coaching1@gmail.com

Website:
www.astrology-coaching.com

YouTube channel and Facebook:
Astrology Coaching by Anatoly

Online Astrology Course for beginners:
https://astrologycoaching.thinkific.com

CONTENT

INTRODUCTION

I found the magic of Vedic Astrology in 2016 – I still remember that day....it was by accident...although wise people say that there are no accidents. I still remember how amazed I was – it was so accurate; it described my whole life. I have been to Western astrologers, but they have never told me what Hindu astrology did...

Since then, I have been studying astrology, and I have been in the field of spirituality and self-development. At the beginning of my astrological adventure, it was very difficult to find resources that I can understand – Hindu astrology was so different from the Western and for a person from the Western civilization, it is hard to understand it...at least at the beginning.

Believe me, it's a shock when you hear that your real zodiac signs are different – Virgo is not exactly Virgo...if you know what I mean....if not, I will explain in the next chapters.

So, long story short, in 2020 I started the preparation of my YouTube channel **Astrology Coaching by Anatoly** and my **Online Astrology course** on the educational platform- Thinkific. I made 50 scripts, which were a result of deep research through my own practice and from the notes I made from people who came for astrological advice, through the books I read, and the multiple courses I had.

Scripts were staying in my drawer, till the moment when Jupiter transit knocked on my door!

So, I decided to combine the whole research and love and effort that I put into my scripts and create a small astrological book, a book for **beginners** or for people who **have never heard of Vedic Astrology**, a book for people like ME, the **"Me"** in 2016.

This is a simplified astrology guidebook, with simple words, a creative approach, simple and easy explanations that will lay a strong foundation for your future Vedic knowledge.

And from that foundation, you will be able to fly...fly like an eagle and conquer the sacred Hindu knowledge.

"Knowledge is the most important thing without which one cannot achieve his goal."

Rig Veda

Chapter 1
Vedic Astrology -The essence

So, let's start by answering the question – What exactly is Astrology? Astrology is an occult science of the relation between the position of the planets in the sky and the life on the planet Earth. Through their astronomical positions, planets determine each person's life and destiny.

That's why the date, the place, the exact hour of birth are very important- we need to know the exact place of the planets, so we can find out what Universe has prepared for us.

Astrology is a part of human existence for many years – we know today about Chinese, Mayan, Babylon, Greek, and Western Astrology, and some of you, especially if you are part of the Western world like me, will hear for the first time about Vedic Astrology.

So, what is Vedic Astrology?

Vedic Astrology is an Indian Astrology, also known as Hindu Astrology or Jyotish. Veda means literally "wisdom", or "true knowledge" and Jyotish means "science of light".

Vedic Astrology is a sacred part of Indian culture and everyday life- astrologers are like some kind of a priest to them. I am always amazed when I have people from India, who want me to read their charts – they treat you with such respect, which is not so typical for the Western world.

Vedic Astrology is one of the oldest astrology- it is the background, the foundation of Greek astrology, which, on the other side is the background of modern Western Astrology.

There are five main branches of Hindu astrology:
- Prashara Hora Shastra
- Jaimini
- Bhrigu Nadi Jyotish
- KP Astrology
- Nadi Astrology
- Lal Kitab

This book, **Vedic Astrology -Easy& Simple**, is based on Prashara Hora Shastra, which is the most popular branch of Vedic Astrology, followed by Jaimini.

In Hindu (Vedic) culture, Vedic astrology is strongly connected with Ayurveda and Yoga. Some astrologers call them "sister sciences". Yoga develops your mental body; Ayurveda heals and harmonizes your physical body and Vedic Astrology shows the map of your life and helps you to fulfill your karma and manifest it in the highest possible way.

Before going further, it is essential for all beginners or people who don't know anything about Hindu astrology to know about the following important terminology:
- Rashi – means zodiac sign
- Grahas – planets
- Bhava – houses of the astrology chart
- Nakshatras – lunar mansions, constellations that construct a zodiac sign.
- Dasha – planetary period
- Lagna – this is the Ascendant/ the Rising sign.
- Varga charts – divisional charts that we use in Vedic Astrology – also known as D-charts- like D9, D10, and more.
- Drishti - aspect
- Yogas – combinations between planets that can be auspicious and inauspicious.

- Ashtakavarga – System of points that Vedic Astrology uses to see what the strength of a house or planet is. All planets give different points to a house – from 0 to 8.
- Moolatrikona sign– a sign which makes a planet especially powerful when it is placed there. Mula means 'root' and trikona means 'triangle'.
- Exaltation sign – a sign, where a planet is extremely powerful. All its qualities are exalted.
- Debilitation sign – a sign, where a planet is considered weak, or its main characteristic is presented differently.
- Own sign – a sign, that is ruled by a specific planet. Planets in their own sign are considered powerful, too.
- Karaka – indicator, atmakaraka - soul indicator
- Chandra Lagna – Moon Ascendant – the Moon in Vedic Astrology is so important, that you must check the chart not only from your birth ascendant but from the Moon, too – you make the house where the Moon is placed an Ascendant, move the whole chart and analyze it as a normal natal chart.

Chapter 2
Differences between Vedic and Western Astrology

After we have explained what Vedic Astrology is, we need to answer the next very important question you all wondering now - **What is the difference between Vedic and Western astrology?**

Indian astrology and Western have many things in common for example the signs and their meanings. Still, there are many differences. In the following few pages, I will present you some of them.

System of calculation

Vedic Astrology uses the **Sidereal system**, Western astrology uses the **Tropical system**. The sidereal system is based on the real position of the stars – the real astronomical system, that NASA uses. That's why this is cosmic astrology – whatever is in the sky, the same is on the planet Earth.

The tropical system is based on the movement of the Sun – that's why some astrologers say that Western astrology is Ego based astrology and that's why the Western world is so Ego-oriented – it is ruled by the Sun, the Ego, and the personality is in front of everything– not the cosmos and nature. That's why there is a big difference between Indian culture and Western culture.

What is crucial here is that the Tropical system uses a **fixed equinox point**, which means that on 21st March, it will always be 0 degrees, Aries.

This means that the tropical system doesn't consider one very important change in Earth's movement, one astronomical process, called **Precession of the Equinox**, in which due to the movement of the Earth, the point of the Vernal Equinox (Spring Equinox) has slowly moved backward in the zodiac - 1 degree for every 72 years.

Yes, I know it sounds difficult- so let's make it more simplified – what I want to say is that the tropical system doesn't show the real positions of the stars, which have changed their places due to the precession of the Equinox. This means that on 21ˢᵗ March, if you look in the sky, you will see that Sun is **not** at 0 degrees, Aries, but due to the precession of the Equinox, Sun is at 6 degrees of Pisces.

Please see the pictures of the sky that I took on 21st March 2021 with the mobile application "Night Sky".

 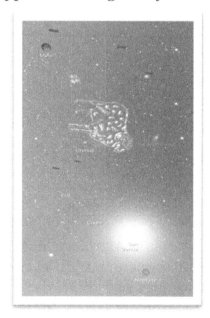

As you can see, on 21st March, Sun is in the zodiac sign of Pisces.

The difference between both systems is increasing by 1 degree every 72 years. This difference is called the ayanamsha. So now it is around 24 degrees.

1900 - 22°28´
1960 - 23°40´
2000 - 23°51´
2020 - 24°8´

This means that all your planets and points in Western Astrology will move backward with approximately 23°/24° (depending on your birth date) and if you are born for example on 13th August 1990, in Vedic Astrology you will have your Sun sign in Cancer, not Leo:

Aries- 13th April – 14th May
Taurus – 14th May- 14th June
Gemini- 15th June- 16th July
Cancer – 17th July- 16th August
Leo- 17th August- 15th September
Virgo- 16th September – 16th October
Libra- 17th October – 16th November
Scorpio – 17th November – 15th December
Sagittarius – 16th December – 14th January
Capricorn- 15th January – 12th February
Aquarius- 13th February -14th March
Pisces – 15th March- 12th April

House systems

Vedic Astrology uses the whole sign house system, which means that every house is one sign. Western astrology uses both the whole sign house system and/or the unequal-sized house system. For example, in my Western natal chart, my first and second houses are ruled by one zodiac sign due to the unequal house system.

Planets and sign rulership

Western astrologers use all the major planets including Uranus, Neptune, and Pluto, and most give the rulership of Aquarius to Uranus, Pisces to Neptune, and Scorpio to Pluto. Vedic astrologers, on the other hand, stick to the visible planets. Visible planets are all the planets till Saturn. Hindu astrologers are using the traditional rulership- Aquarius is ruled by Saturn, Pisces- by Jupiter, and Scorpio by Mars.

In Vedic Astrology significant role, play the shadow planets **Rahu and Ketu** (In Western astrology they are known as the North and South Nodes of the Moon)

Some astrologers are using the so-called ghost planets – Gulika and Mandi (Upagrahas)

In modern Vedic astrology, the outer planets (Uranus, Neptune, Pluto) are used mainly for world predictions or personal predictions if the outer planets are closely conjunct with some of the inner planets. In this way, Uranus, Pluto, and Neptune will affect your natal chart on a higher level.

Aspects

Western astrologers use a different assortment of aspects like conjunction, sextile, square, trine, and opposition, with tight orbs of 10 degrees or less, determined by the type of aspect. Planets only aspect other planets and the angles. Vedic astrologers use a different approach: each planet associates with all planets in the same house, and aspects the opposite house and any planets in that house. Mars, Saturn, and Jupiter also have additional special aspects. Mars aspects the 4th, 7th and 8th house from itself, Saturn – 3rd, 7th, 10th place from itself, Jupiter- 5th, 7th, 9th place from itself.

There is a discussion about the aspects of Rahu and Ketu – many astrologers believe that Rahu and Ketu have not only a 7th aspect but 5th and 9th from itself, too.

Charts

Vedic astrology doesn't use the same circle chart as Western astrology.

We use the North Indian chart:

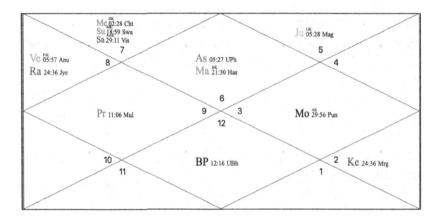

And the South Indian chart:

BP 12:16 UBh		Ke 24:36 Mrg	Mo 29:56 Pun
			Ju 05:28 Mag
Pr 11:06 Mul	Ve 05:57 Anu Ra 24:36 Jye	Me 02:28 Cht Su 18:59 Swa Sa 29:11 Vis	As 05:27 UPh Ma 21:30 Has

According to some astrologers, if you have strong Venus in your natal chart, you will be able to use more easily The North Indian chart, if you have stronger Jupiter, you will be able to use more easily the South Indian chart.

I can say that I agree with this statement - my Venus is stronger than my Jupiter and I find it easier to use the North Indian chart in my analysis, to be honest, I don't get the South Indian astrological chart at all– it is too difficult for me.

Dashas, nakshatras, and Divisional charts

Dashas (planetary periods), nakshatras (constellations), and Divisional charts are typical attributes of Vedic Astrology, and they are not used in Western Astrology.

These are the main differences between Vedic and Western astrology – of course, there are many more differences in the approach and methodology in assessing the strength and weakness of planets, but at this point, we need to keep it **Easy and Simple**. Once, you have the background, you will be ready to dive deeply into the Vedic Ocean.

Of course, if you already feel ready for this adventure, you can always check my Online Astrology Course for beginners in Thinkific, where I discuss in more detail the essence of Vedic Astrology.

Chapter 3
Zodiac signs in Astrology

Main classification

<u>According to the elements:</u>
- Fire signs – Aries, Leo, Sagittarius
- Earth signs – Taurus, Virgo, Capricorn
- Air signs – Gemini, Libra, Aquarius
- Water signs- Cancer, Scorpio, Pisces

Fire signs are more energetic, fierier, more action-oriented, more active, impatient, and impulsive. Earth signs are more grounded, productive, hard-working, practical, and a little bit stubborn. Air signs are idealistic, communicative, and intellectual. Water signs are emotional, compassionate, passionate, and with strong intuition.

<u>According to the quality:</u>
- Movable (Cardinal) – Aries, Cancer, Libra, Capricorn
- Fixed – Taurus, Leo, Scorpio, Aquarius
- Dual- Gemini, Virgo, Sagittarius, Pisces

Movable signs are more active and goal-oriented. Fixed signs are stable, inflexible, and don't like changes. Dual signs are flexible and adaptable.

Some astrologers divide the signs according to their fertility traits, too:
- Fruitful - Cancer, Scorpio, Pisces
- Semi-fruitful- Taurus, Libra, Aquarius
- Semi barren - Aries, Sagittarius, Capricorn
- Barren - Gemini, Leo, Virgo

ARIES

ARIES	
Phrase	I am
Vedic name	Mesha
Element	Fire
Quality	Movable
Symbol	Ram
Gender	male
Rulership	Mars is the ruler
Body parts	Head, brain, the body itself
Nakshatras	Ashwini, Bharani, Kritika
Mooltrikona sign for	Mars
Exaltation sign for	Sun
Debilitation sign for	Saturn

Each of the zodiac signs symbolizes one of the 12th houses of the astrological chart. Aries is the first zodiac sign of the zodiac belt, so it is associated with the general traits of the first house. As you can see from the table above Aries is ruled by the angriest planet in the sky – Mars, so this sign is very individualistic and energetic.

We can describe Aries as
- Impulsive, angry, passionate, and impatient
- Ambitious, competitive, fearless, a man of action
- Stubborn and bossy

Aries is related to:
- Speed and power
- Military and sport- warriors, soldiers, fighters, athletes
- Restlessness
- Temper and ego
- Aries is the baby of the zodiac
- Head, brain, injuries, scars, cuts, surgeries, accidents, fights
- Technical and mechanical skills – engineers, mechanics, etc.

People with Aries Ascendant are pioneers, they are adventurous, proud, love sport and movement, they are courageous, passionate, and intense. Aries Lagna people have great leadership qualities, they can be ambitious and independent individuals. Of course, everything depends on the whole natal horoscope.

The negative side of Aries Lagna is that they can have problems with anger, temper, and Ego, and they can have issues with marriage and finding a place that they can call home. They can have scars on the head or body.

TAURUS

TAURUS	
Phrase	I own
Vedic name	Vrsabha
Element	Earth
Quality	Fixed
Symbol	Bull
Gender	female
Rulership	Venus is the ruler
Body parts	Face, the front part of the head, part of the throat, vocal cords
Nakshatras	Kritika, Rohini, Mrigrishira
Mooltrikona sign for	Moon
Exaltation sign for	Moon and Rahu (North Node of the Moon)
Debilitation sign for	Ketu

Taurus is the second zodiac sign of the zodiac belt, and it is related to the 2nd house of the zodiac chart. Venus is the ruler of this sign- the planet of beauty and love.

We can describe Taurus as:
- Stable and solid
- Trustworthy and supportive
- Beautiful and enjoying beautiful things in life
- Sensual and seeking security in love, money, and relationships

Tauris is related to:

- Wealth, money, and finance
- Resources and values
- Luxury
- Security
- Family, family values, linage
- Culture, poetry, art, speech, music, singing
- Food and nature

Taurus Lagna people are attractive, creative, and have soft and gentle nature. They love pleasures, good food, and beautiful expensive objects. They can be very ambitious, hard-working, responsible, and with high endurance and determination.

Negative traits – problems with early marriage, they can be proud, arrogant, materialistic, and easily seduced.

GEMINI

GEMINI	
Phrase	I know
Vedic name	Mithuna
Element	Air
Quality	Dual
Symbol	Man and a woman
Gender	male
Rulership	Mercury is the ruler
Body parts	Neck, shoulders, hands, upper lungs
Nakshatras	Mrigashira, Ardra, Punarvasu
Mooltrikona sign for	-
Exaltation sign for	-
Debilitation sign for	-

Gemini is the third sign from the zodiac, and it is related to the third house. Mercury is the ruler of the sign – the planet of communication and media.

We can describe Gemini as:
- Communicative and inquisitive
- Restless
- Quick
- Flexible- don't like the routine
- Clever and witty
- Youthful and childish
- Sexual
- Artistic

Gemini is related to
- Media, communication – all communication channels are ruled by Gemini, together with social media and gossip
- Twins and twin personality
- Short traveling
- Friends
- Flirts
- Art and artistic skills
- Hands, hand skills and talents

People with Gemini Lagna are intelligent, talkative, and pleasant. They are like chameleons and change their nature. These people can see things from different points of view but get bored easily. Extremely good at art, craft, and communication.

Negative traits- they are thinking too much and can get overburdened. They can have issues with the nervous system and marriage. They are free spirits.

CANCER

CANCER	
Phrase	I feel
Vedic name	Karka
Element	Water
Quality	Movable
Symbol	crab
Gender	female
Rulership	Moon is the ruler
Body parts	Breast, chest, lower lungs
Nakshatras	Punarvasu, Pushya, Ashlesha
Mooltrikona sign for	-
Exaltation sign for	Jupiter
Debilitation sign for	Mars

Cancer is the fourth zodiac sign in the zodiac belt, and it is related to the fourth house. Moon is the ruler of the sign, and it makes it emotional, but it is cardinal and action-oriented.

We can describe Cancer as:
- Sensitive, warm, emotional
- Intuitive, psychic
- Nurturing, selfless
- Easily insulted.
- Proactive
- home-loving and family-oriented zodiac sign

Cancer is related to
- Home and homeland,
- Mother and the mother figures
- Milk, liquids, and dairy food
- Happiness, joy, and inner peace

People with Cancer Lagna are emotional, maternal, introverted, and attached to their homes. They like to work from their home, and they care about the others. They have great imagination and strong intuition.

Negative traits are their extreme sensitivity. They are very emotional, and this can bring anger and they may feel offended and frustrated.

LEO

LEO	
Phrase	I create
Vedic name	Simba
Element	Fire
Quality	Fixed
Symbol	lion
Gender	male
Rulership	Sun is the ruler
Body parts	Heart, spine, stomach
Nakshatras	Magha, Purva Phalguni, Uttara Phalguni
Mooltrikona sign for	Sun
Exaltation sign for	-
Debilitation sign for	-

Leo is the fifth zodiac sign, and it is related to the fifth house in the natal chart. Sun is the ruler so here Ego and personality play an important role.

We can describe Leo as:
- Proud, like a King, royal
- Love to be the center of attention,
- Leader, dynamic and commanding
- Creative and artistic
- Good-hearted person

Leo is related to:
- Art, media, cinema
- Love and romance
- Children and big families,
- Education
- The heart
- Politicians and celebrities, kings
- Mantras and past life deeds

People with Leo Ascendant can be famous, powerful, and successful. They have great leadership qualities and creative abilities. They may love sports and entertainment, or politics. They are loyal, honorable good-hearted, and affectionate. They prefer to be their own bosses.

Negative traits are that they can be arrogant, impatient, and egocentric. They can have conflicts with others, too.

VIRGO

VIRGO	
Phrase	I analyze
Vedic name	Kanya
Element	Earth
Quality	Dual
Symbol	Virgin on a boat
Gender	female
Rulership	Mercury is the ruler
Body parts	Digestive tract, intestines
Nakshatras	Uttara Phalguni, Hasta, Chitra
Mooltrikona sign for	Mercury
Exaltation sign for	Mercury
Debilitation sign for	Venus

Virgo is the sixth zodiac sign in the zodiac belt, and it is related to the qualities of the 6th house. The ruler is the clever Mercury, and it makes Virgo a great thinker.

We can describe Virgo as:
- Critical, perfectionist, precise, practical, calculative, detailed-oriented,
- Organized and logical
- Modest and helpful
- Clean, diligent, innocent
- Hard-working – they are no quitters, which makes them very successful, too.
- Good at solving problems and conflicts,
- Fighters for society and social reforms

Virgo is related to:
- Health and healing
- Food and eating
- Service work – serving others and society
- Dealing with the suffering of others
- Conflicts, disputes, and lawsuits.
- Fixing the problems, correcting things.
- Daily life and routine
- Virgo in your chart is connected to paying some kind of karmic debt.

People with Virgo Lagna are attractive, intelligent, analytical, gentle, shy, and kind. They love nature and good food and have interests in healing and communication, arts, and education. They can be good at numbers and data, computers – of course, keep in mind that if there is a malefic influence, the result will be the opposite. Virgo Lagna's people are peaceful, sensual, and introverted.

Negative traits are that they can be discriminating, judgmental and overthinking. There can be marital problems and lack of confidence, anxiety.

LIBRA

LIBRA	
Phrase	I unite
Vedic name	Tula
Element	Air
Quality	Movable
Symbol	scale
Gender	male
Rulership	Venus is the ruler
Body parts	Kidneys, large intestines, pelvic area
Nakshatras	Chitra, Swati, Vishakha
Mooltrikona sign for	Venus
Exaltation sign for	Saturn
Debilitation sign for	Sun

Libra is the 7th zodiac sign, and it is related to the natural 7th house in the astrological chart. Venus is the ruler of Libra, and it makes that sign artistic and harmony-seeking.

Libra can be described as
- Beautiful and artistic - values beauty in every sphere
- Compassionate, soft, and friendly
- Popular - Libra rules the masses – this is natural 7th house
- Looking for balance and peace
- Dealmakers

Libra is related to:
- Love and romance
- Spouse and love relationships
- Art and craft
- Harmony and balance
- Justice and courts
- Market, trade, business and business contracts, negotiations
- Relationships between people and contracts between people in general.

Libra Ascendant is considered to be one of the most auspicious ascendants. People with Libra Lagna can be very successful and famous. They can have political power and leadership qualities. They can be good at business, trade, and government jobs. They are social, kind, artistic and creative, frank, searching for truth and beauty. They can have interests in law.

Negative traits are difficulties with marriage and sensitivity.

SCORPIO

SCORPIO	
Phrase	I destroy
Vedic name	Vrischika
Element	Water
Quality	Fixed
Symbol	Scorpio
Gender	female
Rulership	Mars is the ruler; Ketu is the co-ruler
Body parts	Reproductive parts, groins
Nakshatras	Vishakha, Anuradha, Jyeshtha
Mooltrikona sign for	-
Exaltation sign for	Ketu
Debilitation sign for	Moon and Rahu

Scorpio is the 8th zodiac sign, and it is related to the 8th house and 8th house matters. Scorpio is the most karmic sign, and it brings specific karmic events into your life. It is ruled by the angry Mars and the spiritual Ketu.

We can describe Scorpio as:
- Intense and passionate,
- Mystical, secretive, deep
- Stubborn, obsessive
- Sexual, attractive, magnetic,
- Violent and scandalous
- Scorpio is hidden, unseen, and unknown.
- Searching for the truth and unknown

Scorpio is related to
- Death and rebirth
- Transformation,
- Power
- Underground world, mafia,
- Everything that is hidden, unknown, under the ground
- Manipulation and deception
- Psychology, occult, mysticism, astrology
- Depth
- Sex
- Karmic energy
- Hidden wealth, taxes, inheritance

Scorpio Lagna people are intense, secretive, sensual, determined, and magnetic. They need excitement and they love the occult and hidden world. They can work in the medical field, investigations, police, and finance.

Negative traits – these people can be obsessive, revengeful, dangerous, pessimistic, and can have karma to pay in their life

SAGITTARIUS

SAGITTARIUS	
Phrase	I guide
Vedic name	Dhanu
Element	Fire
Quality	Dual
Symbol	Horseman with a bow
Gender	male
Rulership	Jupiter is the ruler
Body parts	Thighs, hips, buttocks
Nakshatras	Mula, Purva Ashadha, Uttara Ashadha
Mooltrikona sign for	Jupiter
Exaltation sign for	-
Debilitation sign for	-

31

Sagittarius is the 9th zodiac sign, and it is associated with the 9th house traits. Its ruler is the guru Jupiter, and it makes that sign optimistic and lucky.

Sagittarius can be described as:
- Philosopher, guru, preacher,
- Teacher
- Educated and wise
- Optimistic, fair, and lucky

Sagittarius is related to:
- Spirituality
- Religion and belief system
- Education, higher knowledge, ideology, theology,
- Wisdom
- Expansion- this sign brings expansion in the house where it is placed.
- Written law and laws of the Universe
- Temples, ashrams, churches, etc.
- Hotels and tourism
- Long-distance traveling
- Different cultures

Sagittarius Lagna people are active, optimistic, love traveling, spiritually oriented, philosophical, generous, and fair. They can be great humanitarians and can have leadership qualities. They can fight for different causes. They can find success in foreign countries. They love intellect and knowledge.

Negative traits – they can be opinionated and promiscuous.

CAPRICORN

CAPRICORN	
Phrase	I do
Vedic name	Makar
Element	Earth
Quality	Movable
Symbol	Crocodile or goat with a fishtail
Gender	female
Rulership	Saturn is the ruler
Body parts	Knees, bones, skeletal system
Nakshatras	Uttara Ashadha, Shravana, Dhanishtha
Mooltrikona sign for	Ketu (as per some astrologers)
Exaltation sign for	Mars
Debilitation sign for	Jupiter

Capricorn is the tenth zodiac sign, and it is related to the natural 10th house in Vedic astrology. The ruler is Saturn, and it makes the sign hard-working and responsible.

We can describe Capricorn as:
- Practical, following the rules and laws,
- Hard-working, serious, and conservative.
- Progress slowly, but steadily

Capricorn is related to:
- Authority, leaders, and ambition
- Delay
- Structure and responsibility
- Government and governmental bodies and institutions
- Profession and career
- Social status and fame
- Life path, karma, and life purpose,
- The wisdom, coming through the real-life

Capricorn Ascendant people are career-oriented, hard-working, ambitious, patient, and successful. They are more conservative and traditional. They achieve their success step by step with slow progress. They want to be at the top of the company they work – the perfect managers, CEOs, etc.

Negative traits – they can be pessimistic, critical, cold, picky, and calculative and they can feel unappreciated

AQUARIUS

AQUARIUS	
Phrase	I understand
Vedic name	Kumbha
Element	Air
Quality	Fixed
Symbol	Water-bearer
Gender	male
Rulership	Saturn is the ruler and Rahu is the co-ruler
Body parts	Ankle, lower legs
Nakshatras	Dhanishtha, Shatabhisha, Purva Bhadrapada
Mooltrikona sign for	Saturn
Exaltation sign for	-
Debilitation sign for	-

Aquarius is the eleventh zodiac sign, and it is related to the 11th house in the zodiac chart. Its rulers are Saturn and Rahu. Aquarius is the other karmic sign in Vedic astrology, together with Scorpio.

Aquarius can be described as:
- Eccentric, awkward, out-of-the-box,
- Independent
- Full of ideas,
- Inventive and scientific
- Social and humanitarian
- Great communicator

Aquarius is related to
- Friends and social circles -all fields connected to networking and socializing
- Society and changing society to improve it
- Large organization and committees.
- Big goals and big desires
- New Age and new technology
- Aliens, UFOs, Aerospace, and the cosmos
- Economy and income
- Astrology and Philosophy
- Communication – PR, media, etc

Aquarius Ascendant people are clever, scientific, philosophical, service-oriented, and great humanitarians. They want to change the world.

Negative traits – trouble in marriage, too opinionated.

PISCES

PISCES	
Phrase	I escape
Vedic name	Mina
Element	Water
Quality	Dual
Symbol	2 fish, swimming in the opposite way
Gender	female
Rulership	Jupiter is the ruler
Body parts	Feet, toes
Nakshatras	Purva Bhadrapada, Uttara Bhadrapada, Revati
Mooltrikona sign for	-
Exaltation sign for	Venus
Debilitation sign for	Mercury

Pisces is the last, 12th zodiac sign and it is connected to the 12th house traits. Its ruler is Jupiter, and it makes it extremely spiritual.

Pisces can be described as:
- Intuitive and sensitive,
- Peaceful and impractical
- Spiritual and creative

Pisces is related to:
- Spirituality and other dimensions,
- Isolation and escape
- Dreams, imagination, and fantasies
- Traveling to distant places,
- Water, oceans, and seas
- Healers, writers, artists, yoga, spiritual gurus, ashrams, monks, nuns
- Addictions, behind-the-scenes and bed pleasure
- The subconscious mind
- Forgiveness and endings

Pisces Lagna people are very emotional, sensitive, and intuitive, even they can have psychic abilities. They can be very romantic, dreamy, and influential. They love traveling and living next to the water. They have charitable nature and can be good counselors, priests, and artists.

Negative traits – too sensitive, they can be jealous, indecisive, high ideals and standards, problems with abuse and addictions

Chapter 4
Planets in Astrology

Planets are the next important subject that we need to discuss on our way to understanding sacred Vedic astrology. Planets also called "grahas", represent a different part of our personality, of our Self.

In Vedic Astrology, we use:
- Sun,
- Moon,
- Mercury,
- Venus,
- Mars,
- Saturn,
- Jupiter,
- Rahu and Ketu- Rahu is the North Node of the Moon in Western Astrology, and Ketu is the South Node of the Moon.

Neptune, Uranus, and Pluto, which we call Outer planets, are mainly used for worldly predictions, country horoscopes, or to see specific traits of a generation of people. However, I have noticed that more and more Vedic astrologers have started to use these planets in their daily practice. Astrology is developing and changing all the time.... It is like a big ocean- new techniques and astrology laws are being discovered all the time.

In my practice, I use the outer planet, only if they are near to the inner planets – for example, let's say that Pluto is 16 degrees in Libra, together with Venus, which is 14 degrees – in this way Venus will be strongly affected by the dark energy of Pluto – there can be big transformations, beginnings and endings through love and relationship.

Let's discuss the classification of planets now.

Main characteristic

In Hindu astrology, planets are divided into different groups:

- **Natural Benefic and Natural Malefic:**

Benefic planets are favorable and auspicious, malefic planets are unfavorable. Malefic is Sun, which is a mild malefic, Saturn, Mars, Rahu, and Ketu. Benefic are Venus and Jupiter- they are "the great benefics".

Moon and Mercury can be benefic and malefic, depending on the influence and position in the chart. If Mercury is next to Saturn, it will have more malefic qualities, than benefic.

- **Exaltation and Debilitation**

As you have seen in the tables for the zodiac signs, there are two very important states of the planets – **exalted** and **debilitated** state/condition. There are some signs, where planets feel extremely happy and powerful, and others where they feel sad, weak, or different. The exaltation state of a planet makes the planet very powerful, and its qualities are exalted and expanded. The debilitated state of a planet makes the planet weak, or its qualities are changed and manifested in a different way.

Of course, there are other states – neutral, own sign, and mooltrikona, which we will discuss too.

In the modern world, to have debilitated planets don't mean that they are completely weak and will bring misfortune. For example, debilitated Mercury will not give you great memory probably or accountant skills, but it will give you thinking out-of-the-box, which is different from the normal.

Below, you can see the exaltation and debilitation of the planets and the degrees, where that states are strongest.

Planet	Exalted	Debilitated
Sun	Aries (10°)	Libra (10°)
Moon	Taurus (3°)	Scorpio (3°)
Mercury	Virgo (15°)	Pisces (15°)
Venus	Pisces (27°)	Virgo (27°)
Mars	Capricorn (28°)	Cancer (28°)
Jupiter	Cancer (5°)	Capricorn. (5°)
Saturn	Libra (20°)	Aries (20°)
Rahu	Taurus	Scorpio
Ketu	Scorpio	Taurus

- **Rulership**

- Sun rules Leo
- Moon rules Cancer
- Mercury rules – Gemini and Virgo
- Venus rules – Taurus and Libra
- Mars rules Aries and Scorpio
- Jupiter rules Sagittarius and Pisces
- Saturn rules Capricorn and Aquarius
- Rahu is a co-ruler of Aquarius, but still, the main ruling planet remains Saturn. The same is with Ketu -Ketu is the co-ruler of Scorpio, but Mars stays "The king" of the sign.

-   **Mooltrikona**

Mooltrikona is the root sign of a planet- the sign where a planet feels like home. Sometimes mooltrikona sign is a sign that the planet rules, sometimes it's the exalted sign of a planet. Here are the mooltrikona signs for each planet:
-   Sun – Leo is the mooltrikona.
-   Moon – Taurus
-   Mercury- Virgo
-   Venus – Libra
-   Mars – Aries
-   Jupiter -Sagittarius
-   Saturn- Aquarius

Please note that the degree of the planet matters in order to determine the power of exaltation, debilitation, and mooltrikona.

-   **Permanent friends, Permanent enemy, neutral**

We have two main camps of permanent friends:
-   Sun, Moon, Mars, and Jupiter – water and fire
-   Saturn, Mercury, and Venus – air and earth.

There are different theories regarding which planets are neutral to each other. Every astrology course I had enrolled told me a different story and at the beginning, I was really confused. I try to keep it with the main planetary camps – Sun, Moon, Mars, and Jupiter are friends, and Saturn, Mercury, and Venus are the other group of friends.

However, I will provide you with a more detailed table of planetary friendship – with time you will understand the logic behind it.

Relationship	Planets
Mutual Friends	Su-Ju, Su-Mo, Su-Ma, Ma-Ju, Me-Ve, Ve-Sa
Mutual Enemies	Su-Sa, Su-Ve
Mutual Neutral	Ma-Ve, Ju-Sa
Friend-Neutral	Su-Me, Mo-Ma, Mo-Ju, Me-Sa
Enemy-Neutral	Mo-Ve, Ju-Ve, Mo-Sa, Ma-Me, Ma-Sa, Me-Ju
Friend-Enemy	Mo-Me

Planets that are **mutually friendly** to each other are the Sun, Mars, and Jupiter. Venus and Saturn, and Mercury and Venus are also mutually friendly to each other.

Mutual enemies are Sun and Saturn, and Sun and Venus.

Mutually neutral to each other are Mars and Venus, and Jupiter and Saturn.

Friend -Neutral - Sun accepts Mercury as a friend, but Mercury accepts the Sun as neutral – the same is the logic with other combinations- Mo-Ma, Mo-Ju, Me-Sa.

Enemy- Neutral - Jupiter accepts Venus as an enemy, but Venus accepts Jupiter as neutral. The same is the logic with other combinations.

Friend -Enemy – Moon accepts Mercury as a friend, and Mercury accepts Moon as an enemy.

These planetary relationships will help you when you have enough knowledge to read horoscopes – the conjunction of 2 enemies in a house, will bring problems related to that house.

Depending on the position of the planets in the specific natal chart of a person, we can classify the planets as **temporary friends and temporary enemies**.

When a planet is placed 2nd, 3rd, 4th, 10th, 11th, or 12th from another planet, it becomes a **temporary friend**. When a planet is placed 1st, 5th, 7th, 8th, or 9th from another planet, it becomes a **temporary enemy.**

The good news is that all Astrology software calculates everything automatically and you don't need to do it manually. When I was studying astrology, I had to check everything without the software- so it was a crazy experience.

Basically, the planets in your chart, depending on their permanent state and temporary state will be classified into:
- **Great friend**
- **Friend**
- **Neutral**
- **Enemy**
- **Great enemy**

These are the 9 levels of planetary strength/dignity:
1- Exaltation
2- Mooltrikona
3- Own sign
4- Great friend
5- Friend
6- Neutral
7- Enemy
8- Great enemy
9- Debilitation

So, the most powerful is exaltation and the weakest position is debilitation. However, please note that everything depends on the natal chart and sometimes a debilitated planet can bring you much more happiness in the modern world, than an exalted planet. I can give you hundreds of examples. Albert Einstein had a debilitated Mercury, but this made him a "different thinker" that changed the world. Debilitated Venus will give you problems with love and partnership but will give you a lot of money, too (depending on your chart of course).

- **Other planetary states:**

1. Eclipses- the reason for eclipses is Rahu and Ketu. They are not physical planets; they are points in the sky.

- **Solar Eclipse** – Sun and Moon are exactly conjunct with Rahu/Ketu in less than 7 degrees.

- **Lunar Eclipse** – Sun-Moon opposition, both conjunct with Rahu/Ketu within 7 degrees.

2. Retrograde planets – in Vedic astrology, they are considered powerful, still, there is some karma that you need to pay, related to that planet.

3. Combustion – when a planet is too close to the Sun, Sun burns it – so definitely there will be issues related to the significations of that planet. Sun eclipses them.

4. Gandanta – when a planet is placed at the end of a water sign around 29/30 degrees or the very beginning of a fire sign around 0/1 degrees, we call it gandanta, which means "knot end" and it is associated with drowning. It becomes a weak planet and can bring some issues. You should be careful with water, sea, and oceans if you have many Gandanta planets.

SUN – The King

Sun in Vedic astrology is called Surya and in the planetary cabinet, Sun is the King. Surya is the creator-without it, there will be no light, no life on the planet Earth.

Main significations:

- The Soul, the ego, the identity, the personality
- Fame, status, professional success, popularity
- Sun is the karaka (indicator) of the Father.
- Power, ambitions, rulership, authority, government
- Confidence, dignity, self-respect, health, and vitality
- Vision, eyes, heart
- Copper and gold, gold color, orange color
- Sunday

Sun is mild malefic because as per Vedic astrology, Surya is the one that brings the human soul to the planet Earth, and souls don't want to be here. Wherever Sun is placed in your chart, this will be the reason you are born, and it will be connected to your mission and karma.

Any planet that is too close to the Sun gets burned. If a planet is placed less than 10 degrees from the Sun, it will be combusted. Astrological software calculates that automatically.

Sun is the natural atmakaraka – the natural indicator of the soul. So, the sign, the house, and the nakshatra that Sun occupies will determine a big part of your personality traits and your mission.

Sun is a friend with Moon, Mars, Jupiter, neutral to Mercury, and an enemy with Venus, Saturn, Rahu, and Ketu.

Sun rules Leo and Leo is Sun's mooltrikon sign, too. Sun is exalted in Aries because the planet of the Ego loves to be in the zodiac sign of the Ego. The King likes to be on the throne. Sun is debilitated in Libra because Libra is the sign of masses, of other people and The King doesn't want to be among the people.

Sun is extremely strong in the 10th house and loses its strength in the 4th house.

Sun rules the constellations – Kritika, Uttara Phalguni, and Uttara Ashadha, which we are going to discuss in the next chapters.

MOON – The Queen

In Vedic Astrology, Moon is called Chandra and it is the Queen in the planetary cabinet. In Hindu astrology, Moon is the most important planet and has the biggest influence. So, we can definitely say that while Western Astrology is **Sun-based** astrology, Jyotish is **Moon-based** astrology.

Main significations:

- Mother, females, femininity, fertility, breast
- Emotions, feelings, imagination, inner peace, sensitivity
- Mind, common sense
- Fluctuations, moodiness, instability, sense of security
- Fame, recognition, masses, mass consciousness
- Fortune, happiness, general well-being
- Milk and dairy food, liquids, fluids in the body
- Cooking,
- Nurses,
- Pearls and silver,
- White color
- Monday
- Sun is the personality, but how you will express it depends on your Moon sign. According to Hindu astrology, Chandra is not only a mother figure, but it can be a cheater, even a sexual player- this is connected to Vedic mythology.
- Moon is lustful – wherever Moon is placed in your chart, there is lust and desire.

Moon phases:

Waxing Moon – Moon moves away from the Sun-increasing its shape in the sky. The benefic qualities of the moon are increasing.

Full Moon – Sun- Moon opposition – very strong and benefic Moon.

Waning Moon – Moon is moving towards the Sun; the shape is decreasing, and it gets more malefic.

The Queen is a friend of the Sun, Mars, and Jupiter. It doesn't consider Mercury, Venus, and Saturn as enemies, still, Rahu and Ketu will always harm it if they are in one house or aspect each other.

Taurus is the exaltation and mooltrikona sign for the Moon- Chandra loves beauty, luxury, and love- all things that Taurus symbolizes. Scorpio is the debilitation sign for the Moon – it doesn't like darkness, sorrow, heavy emotions, and hidden worlds. Moon rules the sign of Cancer.

Moon rules the nakshatras Rohini, Hasta, and Shravana.

MERCURY – The Prince

Mercury in Hindu astrology is called Budha and it is the Prince in the planetary cabinet. According to mythology, Budha was a child of the illicit love between the Moon and Jupiter's wife, Tara. The illicit relationship that Chandra had is the reason why Moon accepts Mercury as a friend (it is Moon's child), but Mercury accepts Moon as an enemy because it is an **illicit** child.

Main significations:

-   Communication, intellect, intelligence
-   Speech, writing, drawing, journalism
-   Education, teaching, publishing
-   Scholars, writers, books, papers,
-   Confidence,
-   The conscious mind and the logic
-   Astrology and the astrologers, mathematics, accountants
-   Skills, analytic skills, skills related to hands,

- Trade, business, commerce
- Lungs, nervous system,
- Healing
- Short distant traveling
- Humor, comedians, witty and naughty individuals
- Friends, classmates, twins,
- Green emeralds
- Sunset and sunrise are ruled by Mercury.
- Wednesday

According to mythology, Mercury is a sexless planet. Budha marries Illa, who was cursed to be 15 days a woman, and 15 days- a man. That's why Mercury is related to homosexual and bisexual people, too.

Mercury is a friend of Venus and Saturn, neutral to the Sun, and accept as an enemy Mars, Jupiter, and the Moon.

Virgo and Gemini are ruled by Mercury and Virgo is its mooltrikona and exaltation sign. Pisces is the debilitation sign – Mercury is practical and organized, analytical, but Pisces sign is too dreamy for Budha, too "out of this world".

Mercury rules the nakshatras Ashlesha, Jyeshta, and Revati.

VENUS – Guru of Demons

Shukra is the Vedic name of Venus. In the planetary cabinet, Venus is the guru of demons. Venus is the only planet that can bring back to life, can resurrect from death. This is the reason why Shukra is an enemy of Jupiter, the Sun, and the Moon.

Main significations:

- Love, romance, marriage, spouse

- Beauty, comforts, luxury, wealth, prosperity
- Jewelry, conveyances, vehicles
- Sexual pleasure and passion, erotica,
- Reproductive system, semen, uterus
- Art, music, artists, musicians, drama, fashion, fragrance, photography
- Mantras, spells, religious rituals
- Harmony and balance
- Legacy
- The marriage partner in a man's chart
- Diamonds and gems
- White color
- Friday

Venus is a friend of Mercury and Saturn, and neutral to Mars. It rules Taurus and Libra. Venus is exalted in Pisces because Pisces is the sign of pure spiritual love, love that doesn't exist in this world. Venus is debilitated in Virgo because it doesn't like to be practical, or deal with problems and conflicts, Venus wants to have love and harmony.

Venus rules the nakshatras Bharani, Purva Phalguni, Purva Ashadha.

MARS – The Commander-in-Chief

In Jyotish, Mars is called Mangal. In the planetary cabinet, Mars is the Commander. Mars is first-class malefic.

Main significations:

- Energy, aggression, impulsiveness, violence
- Accidents, conflicts, trouble, dispute, cuts, burns
- Determination, ambition, motivation, courage, bravery, heroic deeds

- Sport – all kind of athletes
- Military- generals, commanders, soldiers, policemen, guns, weapons, explosives
- Sexual passion, sex
- Medical fields- surgeons, doctors, etc.
- Mechanical and technical skills- engineers, mechanics, builders, etc.
- Siblings and land property
- Temper, anger, fights, arguments, martial arts, blood
- Red color
- Tuesday

Mangal rules Aries and Scorpio, it is exalted in the ambitious Capricorn and debilitated in Cancer. Mars is a soldier and want to be on the battlefield, not in the home, cooking like the Cancer sign.

Mars is a friend of the Sun, Moon, and Jupiter, neutral to Venus. Enemy with Saturn and Mercury. With Ketu, Mars has a special relationship – they together rule the Scorpio sign and have things in common. Still, if Mars is conjunct Ketu or Rahu in a chart, will cause big problems in that house and its significations.

Some astrologers say that if you are a gay guy, Mars symbolizes your partner in your chart. So, if you want to know what kind of partnership you will have, you need to check Mars- house, sign, aspects, and nakshatras. For lesbians- you should check Venus. Actually, in love matters, you always need to check Venus, no matter if you are a straight or gay person – this is the karaka of love.

Mars rule the nakshatras Mrigrashira, Chitra, and Dhanishta.

JUPITER – Guru of Gods

In Hindu astrology, Jupiter is also known as Guru, and in the planetary cabinet, it is the Minister of the Cabinet, Guru of Gods.

Main significations:

- Religion, philosophy, faith, spirituality, devotion
- Wisdom, morals, truth, belief system
- Money, wealth, prosperity
- Luck, opportunity, fortune, optimism
- Children
- Long-distance traveling, foreign lands, foreigners, pilgrimages
- Charity, compassion
- Meditation, astrology
- The husband in a woman's natal chart
- Expansion
- Laws, solutions to problems
- Guru, teachers, priests, bankers, lawyers, judges, ministers, strategists
- Higher knowledge
- Yellow color
- Thursday

Guru is in a good relationship with the King, the Queen, and the Commander-in-chief in the planetary cabinet- Sun, Moon, and Mars. The Guru of Gods is the enemy of the Guru of Demons, Venus, and it is neutral to Saturn. Jupiter doesn't like the Prince of the Cabinet, Mercury, because Jupiter symbolizes higher knowledge and laws and Prince symbolizes fun, humor, flirts, gossip, and normal "low communication".

Jupiter is worldly and expands everything it touches. It rules Sagittarius and Pisces, and Sagittarius is its root zodiac sign, its mooltrikona. It is exalted in Cancer and debilitated in Capricorn. Jupiter loves knowledge, freedom, and spirituality and doesn't like the ambitious, hard-working, status-oriented Capricorn sign.

Jupiter rules the nakshatras of Punarvasu, Vishakha, Purva Bhadrapada.

SATURN – The Servant

Saturn in Vedic Astrology is known as Shani. In the planetary cabinet, it is the servant, low-class people.

Main significations:

- Responsibility, delay, discipline, hard work, restrictions
- Longevity and death, accidents, misery, sorrow, obstacle
- Authority figures, elders,
- Leadership and ambitions; wisdom, that comes from real life, from experience.
- Honesty, spirituality, highest human qualities.
- Organizations, structure, constructions
- Pessimism, fear, worry.
- Low-class society, ascetics, monks, uncles
- Wood, steel, iron, coal, farming, carpentry
- Blue color
- Blue gems
- Good and bad deeds in this or past life
- Saturday

Shani doesn't like the King and The Queen. It is part of the alternative planetary camp, so it is in a good relationship with Venus and Mercury. In Vedic Astrology, Saturn is the most dreaded of all planets. However, in my personal experience, if you are a self-aware person, if you follow Saturn's laws, work hard and you are responsible, you can only benefit from Shani. Saturn will always give you the golden fruits.

A more dreadful planet for me is Ketu, which is moksha karaka – an indicator of spirituality and it will give you lessons, so you can develop spiritually.

Saturn rules Capricorn and Aquarius and Aquarius is its mooltrikona sign. It is exalted in Libra because Libra represents the people, the masses and Saturn loves to be among people. Shani is debilitated in Aries because Aries is ego, ambition, and throne.

Saturn rules the nakshatras – Pushya, Anuradha, Uttara Bhadrapada.

RAHU and KETU- The Outcasts

Rahu and Ketu (The North and South Nodes of the Moon in Western Astrology) are an essential part of Vedic Astrology. They are malefics, which are not physical planets, but calculated points. They are called shadowy planets because they cause the eclipses.

To understand Rahu and Ketu, you should know the Hindu myth about their creation. So, the story goes like that: God Vishnu decides to give the nectar of immortality, Amrita, to the devas, which are the Gods. But one of the demons was so jealous, that decides to change its appearance like a God and drink from the nectar, too, and become immortal.

The demon successfully drinks from the nectar, but Sun and Moon see that this is not a God, but a demon and tell God Vishnu. Then Vishnu grabs his weapon and beheads the demon, but it is too late because the demon is already immortal. The head is named Rahu and the body is Ketu. This is the reason why Rahu and Ketu are the biggest enemies of the Sun and Moon.

Rahu and Ketu are always 180 degrees apart – this is 7 houses -always opposition. If Rahu is in the 10th house, Ketu will always be in the 4th house for example. **Rahu and Ketu determine your destiny.**

In the planetary cabinet, they are the outcasts, and they are closer to Saturn, Mercury, and Venus than the other planetary camp. According to some astrologers, Rahu and Ketu are neutral to Jupiter.

Main significations of Rahu:

- Head without a body
- Always wanting more and more, the best of everything, insatiable worldly desires, possession of material things
- Rahu is ambition, obsession, and desires.
- Manipulation, poison, drugs,
- Immoral, pleasure seeker,
- Fake news,
- Illusion, smoking, addictions, confusing
- Unnecessary fear
- Foreign places and cultures, foreigners
- Chemicals, nuclear power, aerospace, astronauts
- Black and ash colors

Rahu is the future, your mission in this world. It is the head that always wants to eat more –never-ending desires and obsessions. If it is a good sign, this can lead to great success.

Rahu is the co-ruler of Aquarius, together with Saturn. It is exalted in Taurus and debilitated in Scorpio. Rahu rules the nakshatras -Ardra, Swati, Shatabisha.

Main significations of Ketu:

- Body without a head
- Moksha karaka – the indicator of spirituality, enlightenment, and final liberation of the soul from this world
- Non- attachment, asceticism, detachment from the material world
- Healing and healers
- Wisdom and knowledge
- Psychic abilities, ghosts, spirits, occultism, witchcraft, magic
- Loneliness, isolation, unconscious behavior
- Phobias and nightmares
- Poisons, illusions
- Incurable diseases, cancer
- Bad habits,
- Filth, parasites, epidemic diseases, viruses
- Killers, terrorists, destructive actions, mass catastrophes– Ketu is an extreme reflection of Mars.

Ketu is your past, past life, and it will take the happiness and satisfaction of the house that it is placed, to push you towards Rahu, so you can progress and fulfill your mission.

Ketu is the co-ruler of Scorpio and Scorpio is the exaltation and mooltrikona sign, too. Ketu is debilitated in Taurus. Some Vedic astrologers consider Capricorn for its mooltrikona sign.

Ketu rules the nakshatras Ashwini, Magha, and Mula

Uranus, Neptune, Pluto, and Upagrahas

As I mentioned before, in Jyotish we use mainly the inner, visible planets – Sun, Moon, Mercury, Venus, Mars, Jupiter, and Saturn, plus the shadowy planets Rahu and Ketu. However, more and more astrologers are using outer planets, Uranus, Neptune, and Pluto, in their analysis. That's why I decided to include a brief explanation for them, too.

Uranus

Uranus is a planet of sudden changes. It is more like Rahu. It is individualistic, rules electricity and innovation, uniqueness, and independence. It will transform you, destabilize and make you change. Revolutions are related to the planet Uranus – fight for new opportunities and freedom. The house, where Uranus is placed, will require you to change and be independent. If you have Uranus in the 6th house, the house of daily work and routine, this can mean that you will change a lot your routine and work and living place.

Neptune

Neptune is the planet of spiritual wisdom. It is an illusion, disillusion, it is foggy and unclear. It is connected to art, cinema, photography, too. The house, where Neptune is placed, will be "foggy" – there can be lies, uncertainties, unclarity or it can make you grow spiritually and artistically. For example, if you have Neptune in your tenth house, the house of your career, you can become a great actor, photographer, or spiritual leader.

Pluto

Pluto is the planet of transformation, death and rebirth, and power. It is related to the hidden world, darkness, mafia, healing, and big wealth. The house, where Pluto is placed, will be the house of transformation and concentrated power. If you have Pluto in the 7th house, house of marriage, this will mean that through marriage and partnership, you will transform your life or get power, or you can have multiple marriages - depending on your personal chart.

Upagrahas

Upagrahas are so-called ghost sub-planets in Vedic Astrology or non-luminous planets. They are not used by many astrologers. Most of the time they are used only for Prashna astrology, also known in Western Astrology as Horary Astrology.

Main upagrahas are:
- Gulika
- Mandi
- UpaKetu
- Jamakantaka
- Indrachapa

Vedic Astrology software has the option to show you the Upagrahas. These are malefic points that have bad effects on your horoscope. However, I don't include them in my astrological analysis. I use only visible grahas and shadowy planets – they are the ones that influence our life directly.

Chapter 5
Houses in Astrology

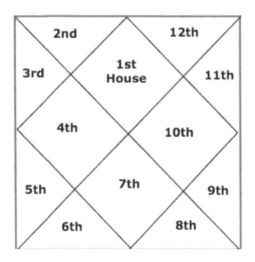

In astrology, we have 12 houses and each one signifies different fields of our life. In Vedic astrology we use the house-sign method – this means that all houses are equal, and every sign occupies a different house. The size of a house is 30°.

You can see in the North Indian chart above how the houses are situated – their place is permanent. So, if you are a Virgo Ascendant, the placement of the signs will be:

-   1st house - Virgo- 1st house is the Rising sign.
-   2nd house – Libra
-   3rd house – Scorpio
-   4th house – Sagittarius
-   5th house – Capricorn
-   6th house – Aquarius
-   7th house – Pisces
-   8th house – Aries
-   9th house – Taurus
-   10th house – Gemini
-   11th house – Cancer
-   12th house - Leo

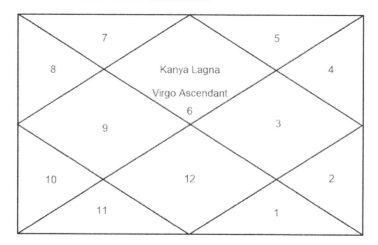

Zodiac signs can be written with numbers, letters, or symbols – so Virgo can be illustrated like 6, Vi or ♍

These 12 houses are divided into a few categories.

Kendra houses

This is the heart of the horoscope chart. These 4 houses play a crucial role in a human's life –the 1st house is – The self, the 4th house is the heart and happiness, the 7th house is love and marriage, and the 10th house is life path and career. They are the most significant influence in the chart!

Trikona houses

Trikona houses are 1st, 5th, and 9th – these are the houses that bring good fortune and luck. The first house is both Kendra and Trikona, that's why the Lagna (Ascendant) is the most important house.

Dushtana houses

Dushtana houses are inauspicious houses- they are related to conflicts, obstacles, death, sorrow, losses, and suffering. Planets that rule the signs that occupy these houses can bring misfortunes.

Dushtana houses are related to the evolution of the soul, moksha, and enlightenment, with psychology and spirituality. One of the best psychologists, counsellors, spiritual gurus have planets in the dushtana houses.

The **third house** and **Eleventh house** are considered somehow inauspicious, too. The reason for that is the concept "**Bhavat Bhavam",** which literally means 'house of the house'. The eleventh house is 6th from the 6th house, 12th from the 12th and the third house is 8th from the 8th house.

Bhavat Bhavam is a concept for people, who are not beginners in Vedic astrology, however, I will give you just general information, so you can see the influences that some houses have – for example the third house is influenced by the 2nd, and 8th houses, too -so the significations of the third house will be mixed.

Bhavat Bhavam for all houses

- Bhavat Bhavam of the 1st house is the first house itself - counted from the 1st house is the 1st house.
- For the 2nd house – the second house counted from the 2nd house is the 3rd house. You always start to count from the house itself – so second house is number 1, then number 2 is 3rd house. That's why the 3rd house shows the effort you put to earn your money.

- For the 3rd house – third house counted from the 3rd house is the 5th house. Let's count again – the 3rd house is number 1, the 4th house is number 2, and number 3 is the 5th house. That is why 5th house takes part of the energy of the 3rd house and this makes it related to art and creativity like the 3rd.
- For the 4th house, Bhavat Bhavam is the 7th house.
- For the 5th house, Bhavat Bhavam is the 9th house, that's why the 9th house is associated with children/grandchildren, too.
- For the 6th house, Bhavat Bhavam is the 11th house. This is the reason why the 11th house can bring some obstacles.
- For the 7th house, Bhavat Bhavam is the 1st house.
- For the 8th house, Bhavat Bhavam is the 3rd house.
- For the 9th house, Bhavat Bhavam is the 5th house. That's why the 5th house is associated with mantras and spiritual rituals, too.
- For the 10th house, Bhavat Bhavam is the 7th house.
- For the 11th house, Bhavat Bhavam is the 9th house.
- For the 12th house, Bhavat Bhavam is the 11th house.

Houses 1, 3, 5, 7, 9, 11 are Bhavat Bhavam for other houses. They will be influenced by the significations and energies of the other houses.

Upachaya houses

Upachaya houses are 3rd, 6th, 10th, 11th. These houses are improving with time. Planets placed in these houses increase their dignity and strength in time and will give good results.

Marka houses

Marka houses are the 2nd house and the 7th house. Marka means killer. Maybe you are asking, why the 2nd and 7th houses are related to death and one of the answers is exactly what we have discussed above -the Bhavat Bhavam concept. The 7th house is the 12th from the 8th house. The 8th house is longevity, and the 12th house is loss. The 2nd house is marka because it is related to resources and food – if we don't have resources, we will die.

Kama houses

Kama houses are 3rd, 7th, 11th. They are related to the things we desire in life- traveling, fun, love, friends, and money. Through these houses, you can understand what in life will make you happy!

Wealth giving houses.

The 2nd, 9th, and 11th houses are wealth-giving houses. Depending on their condition and planetary combinations, you can judge what will be your prosperity and wealth.

Moksha houses

Moksha houses are 4th, 8th, and 12th – they are related to the liberation of the soul. Planets there will show you the spiritual path you have.

Please note that if you want to see the strength of a house, you should analyze the sign, the sign ruler, planets that are placed in the house or aspect, and the ashtakavarga points that this house has – this is the minimum that you must check.

First House – Ascendant

The first house is known as Ascendant, Rising sign, or Lagna – Lagna Bhava. It is related to the natural first zodiac sign- Aries. It is a very important house – this is your chart background. If you have a bad influence over your Ascendant, you may face many issues and challenges in life. Lagna is both Kendra and Trikona house.

<u>Main specifications:</u>

- It determines your whole life – this is the foundation of the chart, this is your entrance to this world, and it is a summary of the whole horoscope.

- Early childhood
- Energy, personality, appearance, character
- The Ego, the Self, dignity, self-love, confidence
- Overall well-being, health, happiness, strength, and longevity.
- How people will see you and how you will present yourself - fame, popularity, status, prosperity
- Relates to your body and head.
- Jupiter and Mercury have directional strength in this house – this means they are strong.
- The natural indicator of the house is the Sun.

A good 1st house can neutralize many of the bad positions, that you may have in the other part of your chart.

The degree of the 1st house is the most important point – it will tell you what will be your Ascendant nakshatra, which determines your personality and mission, too. The lord of the sign and its placement plays a crucial role in the astrology analysis of a chart. Planets that are placed in the first house or aspect that house determine your character and destiny, too.

So, let's take the previous example with the Virgo ascendant:

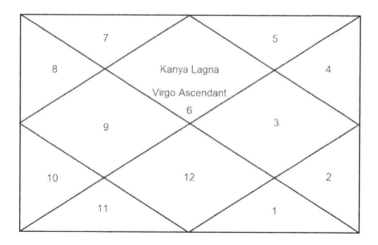

The first house is Virgo, so the chart ruler will be Mercury. Mercury will symbolize you and this will be the most important planet in your chart. Mercury rules 1st house and the 10th house (Gemini)

Venus rules the 2nd and 9th house (Libra and Taurus)

Mars rules the 3rd and 8th house – Mars for a Virgo Rising person will cause a lot of problems because it rules "bad houses" – the 8th house which is Dushtana and the 3rd house, which is a mild Dushtana house.

Jupiter rules the 4th and 7th house (Sagittarius and Pisces)

Saturn rules the 5th and the 6th house (Capricorn and Aquarius)

Moon rules the 11th house

Sun rules the 12th house, so the Sun will have a malefic influence, too.

When a planet rules bad and good houses, like Saturn here -5th and 6th, it becomes more neutral and can give good and bad results, depending on the position of the planet in the personal natal chart.

Every Ascendant, have **Functional Benefic** and **Functional Malefic planets!** As per most astrologers, functional malefic are the planets, which rule, or whose moolatrikona signs are placed in the 6th, 8th, or 12th house.

Functional benefic are the planets:
-   which rule a trikona house of an ascendant and do not have their moolatrikona sign in a Dushtana house.
-   some kendra lords if they are friendly to the ascendant also become functional benefic.

Rahu and Ketu are not included – they are malefic influences.

Here, it's good to share my experience because it's getting confusing. Vedic astrologers have a different opinion about which planet is functional benefic or malefic, there are some discussions and arguments.

What is important for you is to know that **every planet will take the significations of the houses that rules to the house that is placed!**

So, let's say you are Aries Ascendant, Mercury is placed in the 10th house in Capricorn. This means that Mercury will bring the energy of the 3rd house (Gemini) and the 6th house (Virgo) to the 10th house! It will take the good and the bad from these houses! Keep this in mind!

Now I will share with you my **personal interpretation** of the classification of the functional benefics and malefics according to the Ascendant. Please note that this is based on my own observations!

Aries Ascendant
Functional benefic- Sun, Moon, Mars, Jupiter
Functional malefic- Mercury
Venus rules the 2nd and the 7th house, and its influence depends on its position in the birth chart. Same for Saturn.

Taurus Ascendant
Functional benefic- Venus, Saturn, Sun, Mercury
Functional malefic- Jupiter, Moon
Mars- depends on its position in your chart.

Gemini Ascendant
Functional benefic- Venus, Saturn, and Mercury
Functional malefic- Mars, Sun
Jupiter and Moon – depend on their position in the natal chart.

Cancer Ascendant
Functional benefic- Moon, Mars
Functional malefic- Mercury
Saturn, Venus, and Jupiter rule 1 "good" and 1 "bad" house, so there will be good and bad results, which depend on the position of the planets. Same for the Sun.

Leo Ascendant
Functional benefic- Sun, Jupiter, Mars
Functional malefic- Mercury, Moon
Venus, Saturn rule 1 "good" and 1 "bad" house, so there will be good and bad results, which depend on the position of the planets.

Virgo Ascendant
Functional benefic- Venus and Mercury
Functional malefic- Sun, Moon, Mars
Jupiter and Saturn depend on their position in the chart.

Libra Ascendant
Functional benefic- Venus, Saturn
Functional malefic- Jupiter
Sun, Moon, Mercury, and Mars- depending on their position in the chart- can give good and bad results.

Scorpio Ascendant
Functional benefic- Sun, Moon, Mars, Jupiter
Functional malefic- Mercury
Saturn and Venus depend on their position and their state.

Sagittarius Ascendant
Functional benefic- Sun, Mars, Jupiter
Functional malefic- Venus, Moon
Saturn and Mercury- depend on their position and their state.

Capricorn Ascendant
Functional benefic- Venus, Saturn, and Mercury
Functional malefic- Sun, Jupiter
Mars and Moon- depend on their position and state.

Aquarius Ascendant
Functional benefic- Venus, Saturn
Functional malefic- Moon,
Mars, Mercury, Sun, and Jupiter - depend on their position and state.

Pisces Ascendant
Functional benefic- Jupiter, Moon, Mars
Functional malefic- Sun, Saturn, Venus
Mercury- depends on its position and state.

Once, you have enough knowledge about planets, signs, and houses and their meanings, you will be able to understand better the classification. When you start analyzing charts, you will find out that not all the Hindu rules in the books of the great astrologers are completely accurate and everything depends on your personal chart.

Natural Sign-House theory

In one of the astrology courses, which I had during my studies, I learned one interesting theory about the Ascendants and the zodiac signs around the chart. It is a little bit general, but combined with the specification of the personal chart, gives incredible results!

So, let's take **Aries** – Aries rules the natural 1st house and it is related to character, and personality. So, wherever is Aries in your chart, through this sector, you will be able to find your individuality.

If you have Gemini Ascendant – this means that Aries is occupying your 11th house. So, you will find your individuality through the 11th house and its significations: following your dreams, and goals, earning money, and communicating with big circles of people.

Taurus – Taurus is the natural 2nd house, which is money and savings, resources. So, wherever is the Taurus sector in your chart, you can earn money and have more savings, and values. For a Gemini Ascendant, the sector ruled by Taurus is the 12th house. This means that if you have a Gemini Rising sign, it is good to go abroad – foreign places will give you money, savings, more resources, and even you can make a family abroad.

Gemini – Gemini is the natural 3rd house – communication, art, and skills. The house where Gemini is in your chart will be related to communication, requiring skills, or putting effort and courage, doing the required actions.

Cancer – Cancer is the natural 4th house. Wherever you have Cancer in your chart, there will be constant changes like tides, ups and downs. This house will give you emotional security or you will search for emotional security there.

Leo – rules the natural 5th house. Wherever is Leo in your chart, there you can find the things related to the natural 5th house – love, romance, creativity, or fields for new investments.

Virgo- rules the natural 6th house. Wherever is the Virgo sector in your chart, there you will face karma that you cannot escape -conflicts, problems, enemies, debts, and possible healing.

Libra – rules the natural 7th house – marriage and partnership. Wherever is the Libra sector in your chart, this will be what you want in love and marriage, and how you will satisfy your love needs. If you have Libra in the 10th house, it will be important your love to help you in your career, if you have Libra in the 9th house- it will be important your spouse to give you optimism, new belief, help you grow, be guru and teacher for you.

Scorpio - rules the natural 8th house. Scorpio is the most karmic zodiac sign. It is ruled by Mars and Ketu. Wherever is your Scorpio sector, there you will face karmic events and you will need to pay off some karma. If Scorpio is in your 4th house – karmic events related to home, mother, homeland, for example.

Sagittarius – natural 9th house. Wherever is Sagittarius in your chart- there you will find your teacher, guru. If you have a Capricorn ascendant, this means that Sagittarius is in your 12th house. Your "guru" will be connected to foreign lands or any other significations of the 12th house. I have seen that people with Sagittarius in the 12th house, prefer to have courses or go to astrologers, that are not from their homeland.

Capricorn - natural 10th house. Wherever is the Capricorn sector, there you can find status, promotions, life path, and even fame.

Aquarius - the natural 11th house. This is another karmic zodiac sign- it is ruled by Saturn and Rahu. The Aquarius sector will give you income opportunities, making your dreams come true, still, you will pay some kind of karma.

Pisces - the natural 12th house. Wherever is the Pisces sector, there you will search for an escape or isolation, you will be lost and confused. All planets in Pisces feel lost, at least at the beginning of life. If you have the Pisces sector in the 10th house, this means that you will search for escape through work. If you don't like your job, you will need to have an additional hobby that helps you escape and relax. Difficulties finding your life path.

Second House

The second house is known as Dhana Bhava. It is a material house and Marka house and it is related to the natural second zodiac sign- Taurus.

The main specifications of that house are:

- A wealth-giving house – it rules savings, wealth, value, possession, and all kind of resources that we have.
- Jobs related to money, banks, and finance.
- Assets

- Family, family values, traditions
- Security, value system, everything that we value.
- Speech – voice, how do you speak, orators, poets.
- It is related to the face, throat, mouth, and vocal cords.
- Food that you eat, eating habits, and disorders can be seen from here, too.
- Early childhood
- Jupiter is the karaka, the soul planet of Dhana Bhava.

Third House

The third house is known in Vedic Astrology as Bratu Bhava. This is Upachaya house, 1st from the Kama houses and let's say it is connected to some difficulties and issues because it is 8th from the 8th house. The house is related to the natural third zodiac sign - Gemini.

Main significations:

- Communication, all communicational channels – writing, journalism, TV, movies, social media, gossip.
- The way we communicate, the way we do research, and gather information.
- Courage, willpower, bravery, motivation, mental qualities, curiosity, enthusiasm, adventures, and fear.
- Hobbies and interests,
- All activities involving the body- sports, athletes, dancers.
- Younger brothers and sisters, cousins, neighbors, classmates, groups of people that we don't choose.
- Short distance traveling
- Learning, school, education
- Artistic abilities – theatre, music, fine arts, musicians, dancing, singing.
- Handmade art and craft- sculpting, sewing, painting.
- Effort and things that require our efforts.
- Arms, shoulders, neck, lungs
- The soul planet is Mars – because Mars is the indicator of siblings in Hindu Astrology

If you want to have your own business, you need to have a strong 3rd house.

Fourth House

The fourth house is known as Shukha Bhava. It is a Kendra and moksha house. The 4th house is one of the most important pillars, along with the 1st, 7th, and 10th. It is related to the natural 4th zodiac sign- Cancer.

Main significations:

- Home, homeland, environment, security, properties, fixed assets like farms, lands, gardens, real estate, houses, apartment
- The Place where we feel at home, cozy, and comfortable.
- Mother, the womb, the heart, breast, chest.
- The family that you create can be seen through the 4th house
- Comfort and luxuries related to home like cars, boats, and different conveyances.
- Inner peace, happiness, emotions, psychological well-being, mind and thought patterns.
- The grave

- Moon, Venus, and Mars are indicators of this house – Moon is the mother, Venus rules vehicles, and Mars rules lands.
- Directional strength have Moon and Venus- they feel powerful in the 4th house.

Fifth House

The 5th house is called Putra Bhava. It is the second Trikona house and it is associated with Leo.

Main significations:

- Children, especially the first child, pregnancy, childbirth, conception
- Creativity, self-expression, creative energy, art, drawing, and painting– it is 3rd from the 3rd house – Bhavat Bhavam concept.
- Cinema and stage performances
- Love and romance
- Fun, sport, pleasure, relaxation, and recreation
- Intelligence, education

- Speculation business – gambling, crypto money, stock market
- Spirituality, religious rituals, mantras – 9th from the 9th house
- Morals, generosity
- Government, kings, politicians
- Astrology
- Purva punya -rewards from past life karma
- The Karaka of the house is Jupiter.

Sixth House

The 6th house in Vedic Astrology is called Satru Bhava. It is Upachaya house and Dushtana house, too. It is related to the 6th zodiac sign- Virgo.

Main significations:

- Health, diseases, and body functions
- Food, eating habits, preparation of food, bars, restaurants,
- Nutrition, diet, appetite
- Healing and healers

- Medical professionals like doctors, nurses
- Service work, serving others, and serving society.
- Working environment, routine, daily job, employees, workers
- Low-class people, unprivileged people
- Conflicts, arguments, enemies, fighting, competitors
- Divorce
- Small pets and animals
- Litigations, debts, financial problems
- This is the karmic debt that you need to pay!
- The karaka of the house is Mars (war, battles)
- It is related to the digestive tract and intestines.

The 6th house is extremely important if you want to achieve your goals. It combines the discipline of Mars which is the indicator of the house and the intellect of Mercury, which is the ruler of the natural sixth zodiac sign – Virgo.

Seventh House

The 7th house is also known as Kalatra Bhava. It is Kendra and Marka house and it is related to the natural 7th zodiac sign – Libra.

Main significations:

-   Marriage, partnership, commitment
-   Spouse, married life
-   Sexual passion and desire, sexual relationship
-   Other people, the masses
-   Fame and how we influence others.
-   All kinds of relationships and partnerships – business partnerships, too
-   Business contracts and deals
-   Responsibility
-   Courts, market, trade, exchange of goods
-   7th house is a reflection of 1st house– what you are!
-   Karaka of the house is Venus.
-   Directional strength has Saturn – feels powerful here.

Eight House

The 8th house is called Ayr Bhava and it is linked to the natural 8th zodiac sign- Scorpio. It is the second Dushtana house.

Main significations:

- Longevity and death
- Transformation, rebirth
- Sex, sexual strength, sexual charisma, hidden sexuality like gays, lesbians, bisexuals
- Diseases, surgeries, chronic illnesses
- A hidden world, hidden resources,
- Occult, mysticism, astrology, taboo,
- Inheritance, insurance, joint assets, loans, partner's money, the money of others, taxes, will, and legacy
- Misfortunes, accidents, sudden events, disgrace, humiliation, scandals
- Psychology, psychological issues, unspoken emotions, deep emotional issues, endings
- Family in-law
- Saturn is the karaka of the house.
- Reproductive system, genitals

Ninth House

The 9th house is called Bhagya Bhava and is related to the natural 9th zodiac sign Sagittarius. It is the strongest Trikona house.

Main significations:

- Religion, faith, worship, religious belief
- Philosophy, morals, ethical principles, values
- Wisdom, higher knowledge, ideology
- Counseling and giving advice.
- Speaking the truth
- Guru, teachers, priests, preachers, the father as a teacher,
- Grandchildren
- Higher education, laws
- Luck, blessings, optimism, solutions to problems, hope, unexpected luck
- Long-distance traveling, foreign cultures, and pilgrimages
- Terrorists and fanatics, if malefic planets are placed here.
- Publishing
- Jupiter is the karaka of the house.
- It rules the body parts- tights, hips.
- Religious books like the Bible

Tenth House

The 10th house is called Karma Bhava and it is related to the natural 10th zodiac sign Capricorn. It is Kendra and Upachaya house.

Main significations:

- Career, professional achievement, promotions
- Success, fame, honor, social status, recognition
- Life purpose
- The image that we have in the world.
- Government, authority, CEOs, managers, government officials
- Father like an authority figure
- Karakas of the house are Sun, Mercury, Saturn
- Mars and Sun have directional strength here.
- Body parts – knees, joints, skeleton system

It is important to mention that in order to find your career, you should check the whole chart, not only the 10th house – yes, this house is important for your professional path and fame, but you need to check the whole picture and of course the Divisional charts like D10, too.

Eleventh house

The 11th house is known as Laba Bhava, and it is related to the natural 11th zodiac sign- Aquarius. It is Kama and Upachaya house.

Main significations:

- Income and gains, wealth, profits
- Fulfillment of dreams, goals, desires, the house of opportunities, and their realization
- Social networks, friends, professional circles
- Society, elder siblings
- Wild animals
- Big organizations, NGOs
- Powerful people
- Real humanitarians, social involvement
- This is the only house, where all planets are considered good – they grow with time.
- Karaka of the house is Jupiter
- Body parts – ankles, legs

Twelfth House

The 12th house is known as Vraya Bhava, and it is related to the natural 12th zodiac sign -Pisces. It is Moksha and Dushtana house.

Main significations:

- Spirituality, moksha, salvation, enlightenment, final liberation, state after death
- Loss, expenditures, expenses
- Letting go, forgiveness
- Abuse – drug, alcohol, dark places like clubs
- Behind the scenes, secrets, secret enemies
- The bedroom, bed pleasures, sexual pleasure
- Subconscious mind
- Foreign lands, remote places, hospitals, prisons, places of confinement, laboratories
- Monasteries, ashrams,
- Imagination, dreams, sleeping, illusion, fantasies, hidden magic, things that are not real
- Different dimensions
- Retirement, isolation, escape from the world
- Charity organization
- The karaka is Saturn, body part- feet, toes

Chapter 6
Dashas

The dashas are a very important part of Hindu astrology and they are the key to successful predictions. As I said before, Vedic astrology, in my own experience, is the most accurate astrology and the reason for that is exactly the dashas!

Dashas, simply said, are planetary periods. There are many types of dasha systems in Vedic Astrology:
- Vimshottari dasha
- Yogini dasha
- Chara dasha
- Ashtottari dasha and others

The one that I use is Vimshottari dasha, part of the Parashara branch of Jyotish. This is the most popular dasha system. Vimshottari dasha divides a person's life into different planetary periods and every period has a different duration. The sum of all planet periods is 120 years. So, the life span of a human can be up to 120 years.

These are the duration of the dashas:
- Sun – 6 years
- Moon – 10 years
- Mars – 7 years
- Rahu- 18 years
- Jupiter – 16 years
- Saturn – 19 years
- Mercury – 17 years
- Ketu- 7 years
- Venus – 20 years.

The hour that you are born will determine from which dasha your life will start. You should check the position of the Moon and more specifically the nakshatra of the Moon and its ruler. The ruler of the nakshatra will determine your first Dasha.

Below I will give you summarized information about the rulers of the nakshatras:

- Sun rules Kritika, Uttara Phalguni, Uttara Ashadha
- Moon rules Rohini, Hasta, Shraavana
- Mars rules Mrigrashira, Chitra, Dhanishta
- Rahu rules Ardra, Swati, Shatabisha
- Jupiter rules Punarvasu, Vishakha, Purva Bhadrapada
- Saturn rules Pushya, Anuradha, Uttara Bhadrapada
- Mercury rules Ashlesha, Jyeshta, Revati
- Ketu rules Magha, Moola, Ashwini
- Venus rules Purva Phalguni, Purva Ashadha, Bharani

So, if you are born with Moon in Ashlesha, this means that your first dasha will be Mercury because the ruler of Ashlesha is Mercury. After that, you will have the dashas of Ketu, Venus, Sun, Moon, and so on.

The astrological software will calculate your dashas, so you don't need to do it manually. Just for your information, the degrees of your birth Moon will determine when exactly you will start your dasha- from the 1st year, middle, or the end of the dasha.

Every dasha has subperiods and sub-sub-periods. They can reach up to 9 subperiods. In my astrological practice, I use the first 3 periods. The main dasha, which we call Mahadasha, the first sub-period, which we call Antaradasha, and if we want to be even more detailed in our predictions, we can use the second subperiod, which we call Pratyantar dasha.

Let's visualize the whole dasha system, so you can have a better understanding. I will repeat myself, that at this point you don't need to learn how to calculate it- the software will do it for you. We will keep it Simple and Easy...for now ☺

Vimshottari		
Ma Wed	22-04-1987
Ra Thu	21-04-1994
Ju Sat	21-04-2012
Sa Thu	20-04-2028
Me Sun	21-04-2047
Ke Sun	20-04-2064
Ve Tue	21-04-2071
Su Sat	21-04-2091
Mo Sat	20-04-2097
Ma Fri	22-04-2107

Vimshottari		
Ma-Mo-Su	Mon	11-04-1994
Ra-Ra-Ra	Thu	21-04-1994
Ra-Ra-Ju	Fri	16-09-1994
Ra-Ra-Sa	Thu	26-01-1995
Ra-Ra-Me	Sat	01-07-1995
Ra-Ra-Ke	Sat	18-11-1995
Ra-Ra-Ve	Sun	14-01-1996
Ra-Ra-Su	Wed	26-06-1996
Ra-Ra-Mo	Thu	15-08-1996
Ra-Ra-Ma	Tue	05-11-1996

Maybe you are asking yourself, why is the Dasha period so important?

And the answer is that it tells you the timing of certain events in your life. It will tell you when you should do this or when you should not do that. The Vedic astrologers will look at these Dashas to give you the timing of the predictions.

If you are in the dasha of Venus, Venus becomes the most important planet and it will be activated for the next 20 years– its position in the chart, house, nakshatra, aspects, and transits will play a crucial role during these 20 years.

How to judge a Dasha?

- First, you need to know the place of the Mahadasha planet, and Antardasha – the house, sign, nakshatra, whether it's exalted, neutral, or debilitated.
- You need to see the houses that these planets rule – they will be activated, too.
- Conjunctions and aspects that they have
- If they take part in yogas.
- The planet's position from the Ascendant and from the Moon – Chandra Lagna
- You can make the mahadasha planet as Ascendant (move the chart as though it is the Ascendant) and judge the whole chart. For example, if you are in the Venus-Mercury dasha period, you can make Venus an ascendant - analyze the whole chart and see the position of the Antardasha – which house it is now – if Mercury is in the 7th house from the Mahadasha planet, this can mean marriage if it is in the 8th house – period of transformations, 10th- career-oriented period.

Chapter 7
YOGAS

Yogas are a unique characteristic of Vedic Astrology. Yoga means combination – they are combinations between planets, houses, and signs. Every horoscope contains yogas. Some are considered favorable, others unfavorable. Their activation happens through the dashas. Let's see one of the most popular and frequently seen yogas in Vedic Astrology:

Raja Yoga – kingship combination that gives money, wealth, and success – combination/ aspect between the **lords** (the planet that rules the sign) of Kendra and Trikona houses.

So, for example, your fourth house is Virgo, and the fifth house is Libra, and you see that Mercury and Venus are conjunct in your chart (together in one house), this will mean that they create Raja yoga.

Dhana Yoga- this is a wealth-giving yoga. According to Vedic, the 2nd and 11th houses are money-giving houses, plus the 5th and 9th. If there are internal relationships between their lords, Dhana yoga appears:
- The lord of the 1st house is aspected/conjunct with the lord of the 2nd house.
- The second house lord is conjunct or aspected by the Lords of the 5th or 9th or 11th houses.
- The 5th lord is aspected/ conjunct by the 9th or 11th lord.
- The 9th lord is with or aspected by the 11th lord.
- Any type of relation between the lords of the 2nd, 5th, 9th, and 11th houses

- The 2nd lord is in the 11th house, or the 11th lord is in the 2nd house.

Of course, you should check the power of the planets, whether they are debilitated, whether the conjunction happens in Dushtana houses – everything matters in order to see the strength of yoga.

Buddhati yoga – Mercury conjunct the Sun – powerful intellect (if Mercury is not combusted)

Kala Sarpa yoga – all planets are between Rahu and Ketu in a chart. For example, Rahu is placed in the 10th house and Ketu in the 4th house, and all other planets are positioned between the 4th and 10th – this will create Kala Sarpa Yoga.

It will give many ups and downs, and difficulties in life, still one of the most successful people has this yoga because it makes your life story different and unique.

Lakshmi yoga – Moon is conjunct with Mars- it gives wealth.

Vipraeet yoga – malefic planets in Dushtana houses provide good results. When the lord of the 6th,8th, or 12th is placed in another dushtana house, this creates Vipraeet yoga. All bad things that come to you will give blessings to your life.

For example, you miss your flight and lose the money that you have paid for the ticket, but on the next day, you hear that the plane crashed. Missing the flight has saved your life.

Pancha Mahapurusha yoga- when planets are in their own or exalted sign in Kendra house. "Pancha" means 5, "maha" means great, "purusha" means soul, so this yoga makes you great. There are 5 types:
- Puchaka yoga – Mars in Kendra, exalted or in own sign - makes you brave and gives you victory.
- Bhadra yoga – Mercury in Kendra house, exalted or in own sign – gives you intellect, makes you rich.
- Hamsa yoga – Jupiter in Kendra, exalted or in own sign- makes you optimistic, lucky, and fortunate.
- Malavaya yoga – Venus in Kendra, exalted or in own sign- luck in love, gives you a good marriage.
- Shasa yoga- Saturn in Kendra, exalted or in own sign – gives you power and authority.

Parivartana yoga - when planets exchange their rulership signs. For example, Moon is in Leo, Sun is in Cancer. This yoga makes the planet strong. Of course, if the exchange includes the Dushtana house, this can harm the planets and the strength of the yoga.

Kartari yoga – also known as Scissors yoga – when one planet is surrounded by benefics or malefics. For example, you have Moon in the 4th house, but in the 3rd, you have Ketu, and, in the 5th, you have Saturn. This will create Kartari yoga and will damage the Moon.

Another example- you have Saturn in the 4th house, but in the 3rd, you have Jupiter, and, in the 5th, you have Venus. This will create Kartari yoga, but here the effect will be benefic and the effect of Saturn in the 4th house will be more positive than negative.

Sarpa yoga – when malefics occupy the Kendra houses – difficulties in life.

Neechabhanga yoga – a cancellation of the debilitation. When a debilitated planet is conjunct with an exalted planet, or the Lord of the house, where the debilitated planet is placed, is exalted – this cancels the debilitation of that planet.

For example, Mercury and Venus are conjunct in Pisces – Mercury is debilitated in Pisces, but Venus is exalted – this will create Neechabhanga yoga and will give power to Mercury. Of course, it will not be fully recovered, still, it will not be so weak, too.

There are different variants of that yoga, however, in my own practice, I have confirmed that the above-mentioned examples are the strongest options for the cancellation of the debilitation.

Chapter 8
Nakshatras

Nakshatras are the constellations that consist each zodiac sign. Nakshatras, in my opinion, are the most interesting part of Vedic Astrology, because they are related to the Indian Gods and mythology. You cannot be a good astrologer if you don't know the magic of the nakshatras!

The term "Nakshatra" means "sky map"- "naks" means sky, "shetra" means region. Every nakshatra is 13°20´ long and they start from 0° Aries and end at 30° Pisces.

Nakshatras are also known as Lunar mansions because the Queen of the planetary cabinet, Moon, resides in one mansion per day. Nakshatras in your personal chart will give you detailed information about you and your mission.

This is a piece of brief information about the 27 constellations in Hindu astrology.

	1. Ashwini
range	0° - 13°20´ Aries
symbol	A horse head
ruler	Ketu
deities	Ashwini Kumars
animal	Male horse

Ashwini Kumaras are the doctors of the gods, that's why this constellation relates to healing, it is related to youth (Aries is the baby of the zodiac belt)

Ashwini is connected to speed and rapid actions, horses, rejuvenation, medicine, the medical field, ethic, duty, and twins. Ashwini means "the horsewoman".

	2. Bharani
range	13°20´- 26°40´- Aries
symbol	Yoni – this is vagina
ruler	Venus
deities	Yama
animal	Male elephant

Bharani is related to transformation. Yama is the god of death. Keywords here are death and rebirth, transformation, change, dying of the old and birth of the new, burden, and removing of impurities. The symbol is the vagina – the beginning of new life, supporting everything alive. Bharani translated means "the bearer".

	3. Krittika
range	26°40´Aries- 10° Taurus
symbol	Razor
ruler	Sun
deities	Agni
animal	Female goat

Krittika is related to cutting, as you probably suppose from the symbol of this constellation. Words that describe it are sharp, fighting, brave, warrior, and determined. Agni is the god of fire- so fire and fiery nature play an important role here. Translated, Krittika means "the one who cuts"

	4. Rohini
range	10° - 23°20´ Taurus
symbol	Chariot
ruler	Moon
deities	Brahma, Prajapati
animal	Male serpent

Rohini was the favorite bride of Chandra, because of her beauty, artistic talents, and erotic. Rohini means "the red one" and it is connected to sensuality, too. Brahma is the God-creator. So, creation and creative energy are key words here. Moon is exalted here, which bestows happiness, fortune, and wealth.

	5. Mrigashira
range	23°20´ Taurus- 6°40´Gemini
symbol	Head of an antelope or a deer
ruler	Mars
deities	Soma
animal	Female serpent

Soma is the Moon God – this makes the constellation emotional, sensitive, and fluctuating. The deer is a symbol of love and shyness, that's why astrologers connect this nakshatra with love, romance, peaceful nature, beauty, and looking for "food and safety like a deer". Always searching! Mrigashira means "head of a deer."

6. Ardra	
range	6°40´ - 20° Gemini
symbol	Teardrop or diamond
ruler	Rahu
deities	Rudra
animal	Female dog

Rudra is the thunder God that destroys everything. This nakshatra is very specific – it is related to sorrow, tears, and storms. But through the tears, a diamond is made, and through the storms, new green grass is born. Through pain and determination, you achieve success and gain power. Ardra means "moist, green one".

7. Punarvasu	
range	20° Gemini- 3°20´ Cancer
symbol	Bow, a quiver of arrows
ruler	Jupiter
deities	Aditi
animal	Female cat

The god belonging to Punarvasu is Aditi, the Goddess of abundance. This nakshatra is related to prosperity, wealth, abundance, and material gains. It is related to traveling and moving from one place to another, but still turning back to home. Punarvasu means "again prosperous" – the theme of repeating, doing something, again and again, is frequently seen here.

8. Pushya	
range	3°20´ - 16°40´ Cancer
symbol	Udder of a cow or arrow
ruler	Saturn
deities	Brihaspati
animal	Male goat

Pushya means nourishing. This nakshatra is related to prosperity, popularity, nourishment, and happiness. Pushya and Rohini are the most favorable lunar mansions. Jupiter is exalted in Pushya and that's why we connect the constellation with expansion and spirituality, too. Brihaspati is the priest of the Gods.

9. Ashlesha	
range	16°40´ - 30° Cancer
symbol	A curled-up snake
ruler	Mercury
deities	Naga
animal	Male cat

Naga is the Serpent King, the snake that becomes a God. Ashlesha is related to kundalini energy, snakes, hypnosis, hypnotizing appearance, sexual energy and sexual attraction, venom, unexpected attack, paralyzing the opponent, and magic. Ashlesha means "the embracer". Kundalini energy is related to spirituality, too.

	10. Magha
range	0° - 13°20´ Leo
symbol	A crown
ruler	Ketu
deities	Pitris
animal	Male rat

Magha means the great one and Pitris is related to the ancestors and protectors of humanity. Magha is related to family, kings, royalty, traditions, throne. Part of Magha is the most prosperous fixed star Regulus, which is the star of fame and the kings.

	11. Purva Phalguni
range	13°20´ - 26°40´ Leo
symbol	The front part of a bed
ruler	Venus
deities	Bhaga
animal	Female rat

Purva Phalguni means the former reddish one. Bhaga is the God of good fortune and prosperity. That's why we relate this constellation to prosperity and creativity. Bhaga is related to sexuality, and erotica, too. The sexual theme here is more for creating a family and reproduce, having a domestic life.

12. Uttara Phalguni	
range	26°40´ Leo -10°00´ Virgo
symbol	The back part of a bed, cot
ruler	Sun
deities	Arayman
animal	Male bull

Uttara Phalguni means the latter reddish one and Arayman is the God of patronage and friendship. Uttara has a similarity with Purva Phalguni - it is related to prosperity, creativity, and sexuality. However, Uttara is more determined and ambitious - great leaders and people who help society are born under this lunar mansion

13. Hasta	
range	10°00´- 23°20´ Virgo
symbol	Palm of a hand
ruler	Moon
deities	Savitar
animal	Female buffalo

Hasta means a hand. The God Savitar is the Sun God. This nakshatra is related to skills, crafts, cleverness, healing, transformation, hands skills and tricks, magic, palm reading, creativity, and even astrology.

14. Chitra	
range	23°20′ Virgo- 6°40′ Libra
symbol	Pearl
ruler	Mars
deities	Tvashtar
animal	Female tiger

Chitra means shining and Tvashtar is the celestial architect. Keywords here are creativity, bright and shining personality, colors, architecture and art, seductive, and beauty. In Chitra, we can find the fixed star Spica – a star that can make you a celebrity.

15. Swati	
range	6°40′- 20°00′ Libra
symbol	Fresh plant in the wind
ruler	Rahu
deities	Vayu
animal	Male buffalo

Swati means independence and the God Vayu is the god of winds. People born with Swati are like wind - restless, changeable, independent, and adventurous. Air is communication, breath. Good in business, trade, and commerce, eager to learn.

16. Vishakha	
range	20°00´ Libra- 3°20´ Scorpio
symbol	Archway
ruler	Jupiter
deities	Indra, Agni
animal	Male tiger

Vishakha means the forked one and the gods are Indra and Agni – Indra is the God of transformation and Agni is the God of fire. Due to God Indra, this nakshatra is related to bravery, heroic deeds, destroying of enemies, devotion to goals, aggressiveness, courage, ambitions, transformation, and sharp like a fork.

17. Anuradha	
range	3°20´- 16°40´ Scorpio
symbol	Lotus
ruler	Saturn
deities	Mitra, Radha
animal	Female deer

Anuradha means "student of the divine spark" and Mitra is the God of friendship. Some astrologers call this nakshatra "star of success". Keywords – friendship, success, ambitions, leadership, courage, success in foreign lands, away from home. The symbol is the lotus, which grows from the mud of the swamp, and through devotion and courage, it reaches the surface and becomes a beautiful flower.

	18. Jyeshta
range	16°40´-30°00´ Scorpio
symbol	Umbrella or a charm
ruler	Mercury
deities	Indra
animal	Male deer

Jyeshta means "the eldest" and Indra is the King of the Gods- the God who kills demons. This constellation is related to wealth, courage, bravery, the eldest, the one who wins the battle, accomplishments, and authority.

	19. Mula
range	0° - 13°20´ Sagittarius
symbol	Tied bunch of roots
ruler	Ketu
deities	Nirriti
animal	Male dog

Mula means "the roots" and Nirriti is the goddess of destruction. Here you will need to remove the roots in order to find happiness and success. This is another difficult nakshatra – you need to confront yourself, confront your unconscious self. Keywords – roots, destruction, going to the bottom, psychotherapy, remedies, medicine, destruction to create something new, the foundation. Mula is attached to the Galactic Center.

20. Purva Ashadha	
range	13°20´- 26°40´-Sagittarius
symbol	Fan
ruler	Venus
deities	Varuna
animal	Male monkey

Purva Ashadha means "the former invincible one" and Varuna is the God of rain/water. Keywords: invincible, aggressive, water, traveling over water, victory, spreading fame and reputation, influence over the masses, water that cleans and purifies the soul, spirituality.

21. Uttara Ashadha	
range	26°40´-Sagittarius - 10° Capricorn
symbol	An elephant tooth/tusk
ruler	Sun
deities	The ten Vishvadevas
animal	Male mongoose

Uttara Ashadha means "the latter invincible one" and the Vishvadevas are the Universal Gods- gods of qualities such as honesty, ambition, and desire. There is a connection between Purva and Uttara Ashadha. Keywords here are ambitious, victory, confrontation, leaving the past and starting a new beginning, less aggressive than Purva, intellect, and spiritual liberation.

107

	22. Shravana
range	10°- 23°20´ Capricorn
symbol	An ear
ruler	Moon
deities	Vishnu, Saraswati
animal	Female monkey

Shravana means "to hear" and Vishnu is the keeper of the cosmos. Keywords – to hear, to listen, to speak and teach, knowledge, cosmic ancient knowledge, and wisdom, truth, music, sounds, spiritual enlightenment through listening, learning, solitude.

	23. Dhanishta
range	23°20´ Capricorn - 6°40´Aquarius
symbol	A drum
ruler	Mars
deities	The eight Vasus
animal	Female lion

Dhanishta means "the wealthy one" and the eight Vasus are gods that bring wealth and fame. Keywords here are – prosperity, fame, recognition, music, musical instruments like drums, flute, singing, and sounds.

24. Shatabhisha	
range	6°40´ -20°00´ Aquarius
symbol	An empty circle
ruler	Rahu
deities	Varuna
animal	Female horse

Shatabhisha means "a hundred healers" and Varuna is the god of water. Keywords are healing, medicine, secrets, spirituality, independent, mystical, philosophical, meditation, judgement, protection, punishment. Shatabisha means "a hundred flowers" too – this makes people with strong Shatabisha very good with herbs, and remedies.

25. Purva Bhadrapada	
range	20°00´ Aquarius- 3°20´ Pisces
symbol	A sword
ruler	Jupiter
deities	Aja Ekapada
animal	Male lion

Purva Bhadrapada means "the former happy feet" and Aja Ekapada is the god who can transform into a goat. Keywords – unique, different, mystical, energy, transformation, change, passionate, independent, aggressive, fiery, material prosperity

	26. Uttara Bhadrapada
range	3°20´ - 16°40´ Pisces
symbol	A snake in the water
ruler	Saturn
deities	Ahirbudhnya
animal	Female cow

Uttara Bhadrapada means "the latter happy feet" and Ahirbudhnya is the snake that is deep in the sea. Keywords – less aggressive than Purva Bhadrapada, control, anger, charitable, generous, fertility, kundalini energy, mystical, wealth, prosperity, water, coolness.

	27. Revati
range	16°40´- 30°Pisces
symbol	A fish
ruler	Mercury
deities	Pushan
animal	Female elephant

Revati means "wealthy" and Pushan is the god of nourishment and safe traveling. Keywords: nourishment, protection, traveling, adaptation, wealth, hospitality, friendship, animals and herds, spirituality, finding a lost object.

Chapter 9
The Cherries on the Vedic Cake

Jupiter Return

Jupiter return is one of the most important astrological periods. What is a Return? A "return" is when a planet returns to the exact position it was in the sky when you were born. So, Jupiter return is when the transiting Jupiter is moving over your natal Jupiter.

So, let's say that you have Guru in Cancer in your birth chart -this means that when the transiting Jupiter is crossing over your Cancer zodiac sign, over your natal Jupiter, you will have the return of the Guru. Jupiter is staying in one zodiac sign for approximately 1 year, so it is doing a full circle through the zodiac belt for 12 years. So, every 12 years, you will experience the return of the planet. That's why people's life is changing a lot in their 12, 24, 36, 48, 60, 72 age.

Guru is a great benefic, it is optimism, wisdom, spirituality, wealth, and traveling, so every time Guru returns to its birth home in your chart, you will get new opportunities, a new meaning of life, new belief, new ideas, something or someone will appear in your life, that will change it for the next 12 years.

You should start paying attention to what kind of ideas you have, and what people you meet – they will help you align with the higher power and find happiness and fulfilment.

What kind of results, you will have, depends on the position of the planet. If your natal Jupiter is in:
- The 1st house – the return of Guru changes your personality, the way you look, the whole life, give you optimism and a new approach to the world.

- The 2nd house – opportunities for money, family, new resources, new career
- The 3rd house – new business, hobby, courage to follow your dreams, creative deeds, friends that will change your life.
- The 4th house – new sources of happiness, inner peace, new vehicles, home, lands houses, start your own family.
- The 5th house – baby, new business and successful investment, love and romance, a new burst of creative ideas
- The 6th house – a new job, new diet, a new way of living, better health, fewer conflicts, changing routine.
- The 7th house – marriage, partnership, new business partnership, rediscover your spouse.
- The 8th house – a new source of money, you can start your own business related to astrology, occult, psychology, and better relationship with in-laws.
- The 9th house- traveling, a new belief, a new religion, education, revival, optimism.
- The 10th house – new life purpose, new career, promotion, status
- The 11th house – new dreams, fulfilment of desires, more money, meeting influential people and friends, fame.
- The 12th house – healing your wounds, letting go of the past, travelling, fewer losses and expenditure, new deeper meaning.

Please keep in mind that everything depends on your natal chart and above is general information on what you can expect.

I will give you an example with my Jupiter Return. I have the Guru in the 9th house, Aquarius. So here it will activate both the house and the zodiac sign – 9th house is religion, traveling, luck, optimism, education, higher knowledge, and publishing, Aquarius is desires, goals, income, communication, social circle, philosophy, humanitarian, and astrology.

In my first Jupiter return – I went away from home to study Public Relations – education, communication, traveling, new social circles – all are significations of the 9th house and Aquarius. And now, my next Jupiter return is coming – 2021/2022 -Guru will pass through Aquarius again- and the idea of publishing a book in the field of astrology came to my mind – books, publishing, communication, astrology, higher knowledge -all signified by 9th house and Aquarius.

So, now you can see how Guru works – just when you know that your Guru is coming home, start paying attention to the world around you and you may find a new meaning in life.

Sade Sati

Sade Sati is a karmic period, when you will reap, what you sow!

Sade Sati is seven and a half years period of Saturn transition. It starts when Saturn enters the house before the house, where your natal Moon is placed, proceeds when Saturn enters the house of the natal Moon (this is the peak of the Sade Sati), and the last stage of the period is when Saturn enters the house after the house, where your natal Moon is placed. So, Sade Sati is divided into 3 main stages of 2 years and a half.

So, in 2023 Saturn will enter the sign of Aquarius and this means:

- people with Moon in Pisces will start their first stage of Sade Sati (the house before the Moon)
- people with Moon in Aquarius will start the peak period of the Sade Sati (Saturn is transiting over the Moon)
- people with Moon in Capricorn will start the third phase of Sade Sati (Saturn is in the house after the house of the natal Moon)

As I said, Sade Sati is a karmic period, which doesn't mean that it is bad and full of challenges, it means that you will pay for the actions, you did. This period can be a period of great success, fame, and growth. For example, Donald Trump became the president of the USA, exactly during his Sade Sati.

Most often people have 2 or 3 Sade Sati periods in their life. To be honest the first Sade Sati will be always a little bit more challenging than the others – you need to learn lessons that you will need further in your life, or you need to pay karma from your previous lives. So, you will experience a lot of ups and downs in order to learn the lessons.

The second and the third are in your control– if you follow the rules of Saturn, you will receive blessings.

My advice is not to read or listen to any Sade Sati analysis online, without knowing your personal astrological chart, and be careful, who is doing your chart, too. For example, in Indian culture, this period is considered to be bad and if you go to Indian astrologers, they can give you very negative predictions.

To know what your Sade Sati period will be, you need to know:
- the strength of your Ascendant/chart
- the strength of the Moon – house, sign, nakshatra
- the strength of the Saturn – house, sign, nakshatra

- are there other planets that are conjunct with the Moon?
- are you in Moon or Saturn Dasha?
- are you in the Saturn return period?
- are there other planets transiting together with Saturn or aspecting?
- Ashtakavarga points.

Without knowing all of these, you cannot make a real analysis of Sade Sati! If you follow the rules of Saturn – to serve, to help the people in need, to be disciplined, organized, work hard, follow the laws, and real human values, you don't have to be afraid of Sade Sati.

Saturn Return

Saturn's return has the same logic as Jupiter return. Saturn needs about 27-29 years to circle your chart and its Return lasts for two/three years - this is a time of maturity, a time when you will learn important lessons and you will close one page and start a new one, time of alignment with your life's true path. That's why the years before your 30th birthday are very important – you may feel confused, and depressed, and events that happen will make you grow and develop, change.

In order to know what kind your Saturn return will be, you need to check the strength of your Saturn:
- House, sign, and nakshatra
- Aspects and conjunctions
- Dasha that you are in – if you are in Saturn Mahadasha or Antardasha, you will feel the return stronger.
- Ashtakavarga points that Saturn has in this house

I can give an example with my Saturn return – I have Saturn in the 6th house and during my return, I faced some health issues, changed my daily life and the position I had in my corporate job, and of course – I had to do everything with 3 times more efforts.

Mercury Retrograde

One of the most famous astrological events in the sky is Retrograde Mercury! Mercury is the planet of communication, intellect, traveling, astrology, information, logic, business and trade, and healing. Mercury is the prince in astrology.

When Mercury goes backward, retrograde, it creates chaos in its significations:
- Chaos in the communication, media, internet
- Chaos in transport and traveling.
- Chaos in communication between people
- Issues with devices related to communication-telephones, computers.
- Chaos in the information, possible wrong information
- Business-related issues – less profit
- Issues with contracts and deals
- People and things from the past come back

How to judge the Retrograde Mercury:
- You need to know the strength of your birth Mercury – house, nakshatra, sign,
- Dasha period
- Where exactly in our chart, Mercury will be retrograde.
- The houses, which Mercury rules in your chart

Depending on everything mentioned above, some people may feel the effect of the Retrograde Mercury much stronger than others.

When you know that the Mercury Retrograde period is coming, it is better to plan your traveling, business deeds, software update of devices, and contracts in advance.

Divisional charts

Divisional charts are the other important element of Vedic Astrology. They are like a small additional horoscope for a specific field of your life. All divisional charts originate from the birth chart you have. Modern software will calculate them for you, so you don't need to know at this stage the logic of the calculation, still, you should know your **accurate hour of birth**. If you don't know your exact hour of birth, it's better not to check your D- charts.

The most used Divisional charts are:

D9 – Navamsa

It is related to marriage, love, and spouse. Moreover, Navamsa will show you the strength of your birth chart! So, if you have a debilitated planet in your birth chart, but in your Navamsa, this planet is exalted, this will give power to the planet, and it will not be weak.

One of the greatest athletes has debilitated Mars in their birth chart! It is almost impossible to be an athlete with weak Mars! But when you check their Navamsa chart, you will see very strong and exalted Mars. So, you should **always check the Navamsa**!

D10 – Dasamsa

This divisional chart is related to the career. So apart from your birth chart, you need to check Dasamsa, in order to see what your profession and status will be.

D7- Saptamsha

This chart is related to children. So, if you want to know more about your children, you should check D7, too.

This is the full list of Divisional charts

Varga	Domain of Life	House matters
1. Rashi D-1	All areas of life in general	
2. Hora D-2	Wealth/prosperity, yin/yang	2nd
3. Drekkana D-3	Siblings, energy	3rd
4. Chaturtamsa D-4	Happiness, home, fortunes	4th
5. Saptamsa D-7	Children, grandchildren	5th
6. Navamsa D-9	Partner, dharma, soul	9th/7th
7. Dasamsa D-10	Career, power, and status	10th
8. Dwadasamsa D-12	Parents, past karma	
9. Shodasamsa D-16	Conveyances	
10. Vimsamsa D-20	Worship, spiritual progress	
11. Siddhamsa D-24	Education, learning	
12. Bhamsa D-27	Endurance, strength/weakness	
13. Trimsamsa D-30	Difficulties in life	
14. Khavedamsa D-40	Auspicious effects in general	
15. Akshavedamsa D-45	General indications, integrity	
16. Shashtiamsa D-60	General well being	

Transits

Transits are the other prediction method that we use in Vedic Astrology. Transit is the moving of a planet from one sign to another, from one house to another.

Especially important are the transits of the slow-moving planets – Jupiter, Rahu and Ketu and Saturn. These planets will always change the energy in your life, I call them "The Big Changers."

How to judge a transit?

- First, you need to know your Dasha period – the planet of your Mahadasha and Antardasha are the most important planets for that period of your life – so for example, if you are in Saturn mahadasha, you can feel the transit of Shani up to 100%, because Saturn is the most important planet for you at this moment. As I said, the Mahadasha planet determines what events will happen in your life and we should follow the transits of that planet, not only analyze its birth position. If you are in Venus- Mercury period, for example, you will still feel the transits of Jupiter, Saturn, Rahu and Ketu, but not so strong – 30-50% , depending on all other factors in your chart, because the most important will be the transits of Venus and Mercury for you! This is why there are so many people who are saying, for example, I have transit of Jupiter in the 11th house, but I didn't get a lot of money...you don't get a lot of money maybe because you are not in the Dasha of Jupiter or because your birth Jupiter is weak.

- You need to see the whole birth chart and the natal positions of your planets – houses, conditions, exaltations, debilitations, nakshatras, conjunctions, and yogas. It is different when Saturn is transiting over your natal Moon and Saturn transiting over an empty house.

- You need to know the Ashtakavarga points that the transiting planet gives to a house – if they give the maximum, 8 points, the transit will be good, but if it gives 0 points, the transit will be bad.

- **Always** check the transits from your **Ascendant** and your Moon- **Chandra Lagna**. As per my own experience, transits looked from the Moon are more karmic and destined, while the transits checked from the Ascendant are related to opportunities that you can receive, but they totally depend on you – whether you are willing to do the actions and put the effort!

Chapter 10
Horoscope example

Let's take this example and discuss it, the planet information is below:

	Degrees	nakshatra
Ascendant	12° Gemini	Ardra
Sun	2° Virgo	Uttara Phalguni
Moon	26° Pisces	Revati
Mercury	7° Gemini	Ardra
Venus	14° Libra	Swati
Saturn	10° Scorpio	Anuradha
Mars	27° Sagittarius	Uttara Ashadha
Jupiter	29° Aquarius	Purva Bhadrapada
Rahu	29° Pisces	Revati
Ketu	29 ° Virgo	Chitra

So, what do we see?

Let's make one brief analysis of the chart!

First, this person is a Gemini Ascendant, and the ruler of the chart, which is the ruler of the Rising zodiac sign, is in the 1st house – in its own sign. Mercury feels like home in Gemini, moreover, Mercury feels powerful in the first house. This is a great position for Mercury and, as I said before when the Ascendant and the ruler of the Ascendant are strong, then the person will have the power to overcome all the troubles and misfortunes.

Communication, intellect, speech, traveling, fun and humor, youthfulness, great businessman – all these will describe such a person. The Ascendant is **You**- a mix of the traits of the zodiac sign, the ruler, the nakshatra and the ruler of the nakshatra, and all planets, placed in the Ascendant or aspecting it.

The nakshatra Ardra is a little bit troublesome, but still, if you want a rainbow, you must be ready for the rain. There will be a lot of transformations. I can say for sure that this person will love wearing green colors – Mercury is green, Ardra is green, and fresh grass, so for sure he or she will look young, cheerful, and vibrant. Dogs will give them power and luck – the dog is the symbol of Ardra. It's good to have green plants and herbs in the house.

The first house is the Self, the personality, the power, and fame – so I am pretty sure such a person will become famous through communication, intellect or business.

Mercury is aspected by Mars and Jupiter – as you know Mars and Jupiter have special aspects – Mars aspect the house 4th, 7th, 8th by its place and Jupiter-5th, 7th, 9th from its place. This will make that person energetic, ambitious, opinionated, lucky, will need to pay attention how to behave, especially with the spouse.

Mars and Jupiter are not friends with Mercury, so this person will need to find balance with the aggression, energy and learn how to communicate in the right way – Jupiter is higher knowledge and Mercury is a more casual communication style.

The second house is Cancer and it's empty. When a house is empty, we need to see the ruler and the aspects – the ruler is Moon and it's in the 10th house together with Rahu. There will be a lot of ups and downs in the financial and family field. Wherever is the Cancer in your chart, you can expect tides! Still, this person will earn money through career and profession. Rahu is an enemy of the Moon.

The third house is Leo, the ruler is in the 4th house. The 3rd house is aspected by Saturn with its 10th aspect. Saturn is the other planet with special aspects – 3rd, 7th, 10th from itself. This means that this person will be artistic, will have lion-like communication, and Saturn will make that person put effort and work hard. Jupiter aspects the house with its 7th aspect, so spiritual communication, teaching and preaching others.

Sun and Ketu in Virgo in 4th house – this will create issues! First, Sun is weak in the 4th house, it doesn't have directional strength, it is with its enemy- the Body without head, Ketu. So maybe the first part of life, this person will need to find the Self, heal the Ego, find his/her real personality and what he or she wants. People with Sun in 4th house, succeed in their second part of life.

Ketu in 4th with Sun, Rahu in 10th with Moon tells that there will be problems with mother and father and the relationship between them. Sun is the father, which is harmed by Ketu, Moon is the mother, which is harmed by Rahu, this person is even born on Moon eclipse. Definitely karmic relationship with the family.

The good news is that Sun is in its own nakshatra - Uttara Phalguni. This will give power to the Sun and make that person more artistic, even sexual. Sun and Ketu are not close in degrees, too, which will decrease the bad effect of the conjunction. The closer are planets- the stronger is the conjunction!

Ketu will take the satisfaction from the 4th house – home, inner peace and happiness, mother and will make you move towards Rahu. You will not be happy living in your homeland – most probably you will live abroad or far away from your home.

The ruler of the 4th house is Mercury, and Mercury is in 1st house – so the home will influence your whole personality or even you can have a business related to home, mother, inner peace and happiness.

The 5th house is Libra and Venus is there – so Venus is in its own sign, which makes the planet strong. Love, romance, new investments, beautiful self-expression. Jupiter aspect Venus with its 9th aspect. You will need love and romance in your relationship. Beauty will be important for you not only in partnership but in your environment. Venus rules the 12th house, too – the house of losses, foreign lands – there can be some loss around love or love affairs abroad.

The issue here is the Scissor yoga – Venus is surrounded by Ketu, Sun, and Saturn – this will suppress the benefic influence of Venus a little bit.

The 6th house is ruled by Scorpio and Saturn is placed there. Basically, the malefic planet feels good in Dushtana houses – "minus and minus" is a plus. Saturn here will make you work nonstop, but it will make you non-quitter. This is a great position for ambitious persons because the planet of hard work is in the house of routine work. People with such a position should pay attention to the fun side of life, too. Saturn will give good health with time. Saturn is in Scorpio, which is ruled by Mars, and it doesn't feel happy- this can create tension, conflicts and enemies. However, this is a Upachaya house and with time things will get better. Saturn is in its own nakshatra, too.

Saturn rules Capricorn and Aquarius – 8th and 9th house – father can become an enemy here. We see Vipraeet yoga – the lord of the 8th is in the 6th. This can bring a sudden rise in life.

The 7th house is Sagittarius and Mars is placed here. Mars receives an aspect from Mercury - problems, a power struggle with the spouse, conflicts, emotional issues with the spouse. However, Mars is in a friendly sign. Sagittarius is ruled by Jupiter, which will mild the anger of Mars. This person for sure has a strict belief system and ideals. We see what kind of spouse, this person will have, from the 7th house –the spouse will be athletic, educated, loves traveling and knowledge.

The issue here is that Mars rules the 6th house and 11th house – all bad houses for a Gemini Ascendant. Mars is a first-class malefic for Gemini Rising. So, we can expect conflicts, even divorce with the spouse, due to miscommunication most probably. However, the 11th house is income and desires, so maybe through marriage, this person can fulfil his/her goals.

The 8th house is Capricorn and there are no planets there. Saturn is the ruler and as I said it creates Vipraeet yoga. Capricorn is slow, heavy, hard-working and in the 8th, house can mean that you will live longer, and you will experience fewer sudden changes. The 9th house is Aquarius, and Jupiter is there. Jupiter is neutral to Saturn and in Aquarius it will expand your knowledge, communication, and organizational skills. For sure you will be a good advisor and counsellor. Often you can see spiritual coaches and gurus with Jupiter in Aquarius.

Jupiter rules the 7th and 10th house – so you need to check this planet to know more about your partner and career. Definitely, you will need an educated and clever partner, who can help you grow in your profession and status in society, partner with opinion, partner, who likes traveling.

The 10th house is the Pisces sign, Moon and Rahu are placed there. Two very important planets – Moon is the most significant planet in Vedic astrology- it shows your emotional world and your well-being. Rahu is your mission – the house where Rahu is placed, show you what you need to do in your life. The lord (the ruler) of the 10th house, Jupiter, is in the 9th – which means luck, good education, strong belief system. However, Moon and Rahu conjunction creates a lot of problems:

-   First, Moon is aspected from many planets – Sun, Ketu, Mars, and conjunct with Rahu – all "malefics". Definitely, there will be depressions, emotional turmoil, maybe suicidal thoughts.
-   Rahu and Moon conjunction is a combination for fame – so this person can become very famous. **Wherever is the Moon, there is the mind, wherever is Rahu, there is the mission** and the insatiable hunger – obsession with career.

Always check the nakshatras of the planets, especially the one of the Ascendant, Moon and the Dasha planet! Moon in Revati will make you a protector, will make you care about other people and animals. It's good to live in a place near water, sea, oceans.

The 11th house is Aries and its empty. Mars is the lord of the house and it's in the 7th house – money through partnership. Venus is aspecting it- women can bring money to your life.

The 12th house is Taurus, and the ruler Venus is in the 5th house, own sign. Love of travelling. Going abroad will be important for earning money. Taurus is the natural second house, house of money and savings, so wherever your Taurus is, there you can find your wealth. This is too general of course, but still, it resonates with most of the charts I have seen.

So, this is a general explanation of a chart – you need to check many other factors like the Chandra Lagna, the Navamsa chart, Ahstakavarga points, the rulers of the nakshatras and their placement, the other divisional charts, so you can confirm the full potential of the horoscope.

Chandra Lagna is when you make the sign of the Moon as an Ascendant. It is very important Lagna – it shows your emotional world, well-being and describes your personality in an even more detailed way. The Chandra Lagna of this chart will be:

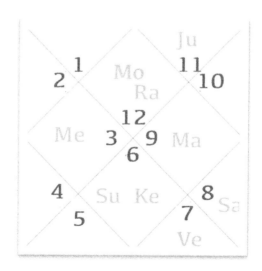

The dashas

Moon in the natal chart is placed in Revati, which means that your first Dasha will be Mercury. After that Ketu, Venus, Sun, Moon, Mars, Rahu, Jupiter, Saturn.

So if this person is in Venus dasha, this means that from the Ascendant Venus is in 5th house, from the Moon it is in 8th house- Venus is in Libra, ruling Taurus – we can expect on one hand themes related to love, romance, education, going abroad, foreign love affairs or more expenditures, but still a lot of transformation and sudden events in love and life, due to the 8th place of the Mahadasha planet in the Chandra Lagna! Beauty will be important – you will need beauty and harmony. This is just a brief explanation. We need to check much more things in order to be specific. I just want to show you, how it works.

It is good to make Venus an Ascendant and do an analysis of the chart, too – it will give you further details about the Mahadasha period.

Especially useful is to check the position between the Mahadasha planet and the antardasha. For example, you are in the Venus- Jupiter period – this means that Jupiter is in the 5th house from the Mahadasha planet- please refer to the chart above. In this period, you can expect events related to the 5th house, too -love, romance, education, children, new investments. Of course, you need to look and the real ascendant and Moon Lagna, too.

If you are in Venus mahadasha and Sun antardasha, you can expect events related to the 12th house matters, because Sun is placed in the 12th house from the Mahadasha planet – losses, expenditures, foreign lands and traveling.

Conclusion

Vedic Astrology has been known on Earth for thousands of years. It is one of the most ancient astrologies – this is an astrology, where myths, legends and wisdom come together!

And this is the astrology that chose me.... let say it in this way. I think there is some kind of karma.... Jyotish means "Science of light" and my name in Greek means "East" or "the place, where Sun rises."

Vedic Astrology – Easy& Simple is structured and written in an easy and simple way, so people from the Western world can understand it. It represents a good background, on which you can step and go further in your astrology enlightenment. As I said in the introduction part, the aim of the book is to help beginners and people, who have never heard about Jyotish, just like I was in 2016.

I even made a special notebook for all Hindu students - **Vedic Astrology – Easy& Simple-The Notebook-** which you can find in Amazon. This is the first notebook in Vedic Astrology with drawn North and South Indian charts, that can help you with your Vedic studies.

I have had many astrology courses, read many books in this field, I struggled a lot to find the right resources and information, so that's why I wanted to help all Vedic astrology beginners and managed even to create a special **online video astrology course**, called **Online Astrology Course for Beginners** in the platform Thinkific.

It is a much more extended and detailed video version of my book. It is interesting, and it is created especially for the new students of Vedic astrology and for people, who wants to read their charts alone, without searching for other astrologers.

In the **Online Astrology Course for Beginners** I discuss in an Easy and Simple way (like the book) the foundation of Jyotish- signs, houses, planets, dashas, transits, nakshatras, yogas, D-charts, I even go further – I show you how to read the chart, the conjunctions, how to see important events in your life like children, promotions, finding love, marriage, synastry, how to read chart of a country (Mundane Astrology), Jaimini astrology, give you a lot of examples.

In order to dive deeply into the ocean of Hindu astrology, first, you need to know how to swim, right? So, if you want to study astrology, check my course online or through this link:

https://astrologycoaching.thinkific.com

Helpful recommendations:

Here, I will give you some pieces of advice:

- One big mistake that I made at the beginning, is that I started reading books from different branches of Jyotish- I read about Prashara, Jaimini, KP Astrology and even Nadi – a huge mistake! Keep it Simple – start with only one branch – first, learn Prashara, then you can start with Jaimini or the other way around.

- Do not mix at least at the beginning the Vedic and Western astrology!

- Be careful how much money you give for courses – it is full of expensive astrological courses that cost thousands of dollars and they are nothing special and unique. If you have the astrological talent in your natal chart – believe me, you don't need to spend so much money. Everybody knows the main principles and knowledge- but not everyone has the Connection – the connection with the Ether, the Cosmos, not everybody has the intuition to read the chart.

No course can give you this connection!

- Choose wisely the astrologers you visit or follow- some of them, especially the one online- on TV, YouTube and social media, are not what they seem to be.

- The Vedic astrologers from India have a totally different approach, compared to the Western Vedic astrologers. My advice is, if you come from the Western world, first, start your Hindu education with Western Vedic astrologers.

- Believe in your intuition! This is the compass of the Universe that is engraved in your heart.

- My favorite Vedic astrological software is Parashara's lights – the screenshots that you have seen in some of the chapters are from this software. This is not an advertisement – I don't receive anything for mentioning it, just want to support you on your way of spiritual development.
- I can recommend you read books written by Richard Fish and Rayan Kurczak, Joni Patry, Kapiel Raaj, James Braha, David Frawley. They are written in an easy way and give deeper knowledge.

- Every astrologer has his own style – you should choose your most favorite approach, methods, branch and turn it in your **own astrology brand**!

- I realized that some astrologers, especially on YouTube can be very good astrology teachers and Gurus, but in the real practice with people, they can be just average. Some are meant to be teachers; others are meant to be counsellors and healers!

- Never destroy the **Hope and Belief** of your future clients, that they can achieve what their heart desires – there are always different ways to say some not very positive prediction and still tell the truth. You should be the perfect communicator!

Hope and Belief can do miracles!

- Never take for granted the people who come to you for help – their hearts have pain, and you should respect that pain!

- The Vedic traditional astrological remedies are not working efficiently on people, who don't have anything in common with Hindu religion, traditions, and culture!

- If you want to be a popular astrologer online – it's easier to be part of the mainstream- the masses don't understand the real wisdom of the astrology – they want to hear daily horoscopes, weekly horoscopes, what is the best zodiac sign, what is the worst zodiac signs and so on. But I recommend you not to choose the mainstream, it will be more difficult, still, I advise you to **be yourself** and to do things that you really believe in!

The magic is to have profound knowledge, but to keep it **Easy and Simple**! The real-life beauty is in the simple things.... this is the reason that I created my book and online astrology course- Easy and Simple!

About the Author

Anatoly Malakov is a certified Vedic astrologer, author, YouTuber, and spiritual coach. He combines the magic of Vedic Astrology with practical spiritual coaching and manifests his own "Astrology Coaching" spiritual practice. He believes that astrology is like a map that shows us the path and the future, however, we people still have free will. Through astrological coaching, we can take the most from our lives and fulfil our dreams.

Anatoly Malakov is the author of the "Easy & Simple" series for beginners in Vedic astrology:
- "Vedic Astrology- Easy&Simple" (book)
- "Vedic Astrology- Easy&Simple- The Notebook"
- "Nakshatras in Vedic Astrology – Easy&Simple"
- "Nakshatras Journal"

He is the author of spiritual coaching journals like:
- Coloring Gratitude Journal: The Power of Gratitude Combined with Color Therapy and Positive Affirmations
- Diario de gratitud y Colorear (Spanish edition)
- Dating Journal: Rate and Assess Your Love Dates

He is the creator of a special simplified Vedic astrology course for beginners with pre-recorded videos, which is the online continuation of the "Easy&Simple" approach.

Online Video Course for beginners in Vedic Astrology - https://astrologycoaching.thinkific.com/

For contact and horoscope readings, please refer to:
- website - https://astrology-coaching.com/
- email: astrology.coaching1@gmail.com
- YouTube – Astrology Coaching by Anatoly

"Astrology for me is like a map – it shows you what to expect if you choose that road or other...it will tell you, you need to take a jacket, it will be cold on that road....and it will tell you, take sunglasses...it will be fun now...but what is most important, you have to walk the way.

*Some people think that they can stay on the couch and wait for the karma....no, you are here to "**move**" and only through moving....you can complete your dharma, your mission.*

Some events are destined, they are karmic, there are lessons that you cannot avoid and still, there is free will and when you learn the lessons, then you can achieve everything you desire and want.

When you are a spiritually aware person and you know yourself and your emotional world, you can control your destiny and use astrology as a map that can guide you....but please....

MOVE*...."*

Anatoly Malakov

Made in United States
North Haven, CT
28 June 2025

70197091R10078